Until a Dead Horse Kicks You

Until a Dead Horse Kicks You

The Story of an Ordinary Hero
Alec Griffiths 1900–1995

Robert Crack

Kangaroo Press

First published in Australia in 2000 by Kangaroo Press
an imprint of Simon & Schuster (Australia) Pty Limited
20 Barcoo Street, East Roseville NSW 2069

A Viacom Company
Sydney New York London Toronto Tokyo Singapore

National Library of Australia
Cataloguing-in-Publication data

Crack, Robert.

Until a dead horse kicks you: the story of an ordinary hero Alec Griffiths 1900–1995

Includes index.
ISBN 0 7318 1015 5.
1. Griffiths, Alec, 1900-1995 2. Australia. Army. Australian Flying Corps - Biography. 3. Airmen - Australia - Biography. 4. World War, 1914–1918 - Aerial operations, Australian. I. Title I. Title : Story of Alec Griffiths.

940.544994

Cover design by Gayna Murphy, Greendot Design

Set in Sabon 11/14.7
Printed by Griffin Press

10 9 8 7 6 5 4 3 2

Contents

To Effie
and our children,
and to Grafton, which was the making of me.
A.G.

Author's note

There will come a time, years from now, when my children — if there are any — will learn about the conflict once called the war that will end war. When they ask me what I know of the Great War, there will be no need to cite dates, places and historical accounts. It will be enough to say, 'I knew an Australian Digger. He was a good cobber of mine, actually.'

Alec Griffiths died on 11 April 1995, just a handful of days before his seventy-sixth Anzac Day.

Although the words which follow come from my pen, this is as much Alec's story as it is my book. Based on oral testimony it is the story of an ordinary, and at once remarkable man, who witnessed the better part of the twentieth century. He also witnessed the worst.

Just as he dedicates his story to his wife and children, I in turn dedicate my book to him.

R.C.

Silent and purposeful, through a field of chalky white, he shuffled. He glided to a halt as he found the object for which he had been searching. The journey here had been long, the route trying. The mud of the track that led here had covered his feet for seventy-five years.

There were no tears. No. The spongy soil of this land was already soaked through with tears, and could bear no more. Before him, the earth divulged its long-kept secret.

PART I

THE EARLY YEARS

CHAPTER ONE
Vale William

The sudden breeze plucked a few lingering leaves of autumn from the ground. It whispered to the fruit trees by the pond and sent the leaves barrelling off into the dusty air. Their loss would be lamented by the people who lived at the house. In the parched, unforgiving land they knew as New South Wales — where rare autumn leaves were a smudge on the canvas of eucalyptus — the departure of such precious reminders of southern Wales would always be a small sadness.

A dainty picket fence enclosed the small garden. It had tried, and failed, to make the Welsh farmer feel at home. The vegetables in the garden always succumbed to the sun. The watercourse that meandered down in front of the homestead — so long as rains came every now and again — would never be more than a muddy trickle. And the whitewashed mud brick walls of the cottage at 'Shaftsbury' had been baked as hard as iron by the sun of a land on which an iron will was needed just to survive.

William Griffiths was a man of such will. The constant support of his dear wife Eliza Jane had made sure of it. But an iron will was no match for sickness in these parts, where help was often days away.

Thirteen-year-old Hilda Griffiths, her heart in her mouth, hurried home from school that day in April 1905, as she had been doing every day for the past few weeks. Her downcast eyes searched the track for the wheel ruts that may have been left behind by a cart. Her anxiety was almost unbearable. Beside her, Alec, who adored his older sister and was never far from her heels, was also worried. He wasn't sure why, but if Hilda was worried then so was he.

'Where's Daddy, Hilda?'

In the distance the wheel ruts converged like an arrowhead in the direction of Cootamundra. 'They've taken him into town,' Hilda replied, bursting into tears.

Their father had not been himself of late. One day Alec had gone outside to investigate what sounded like a distressed animal. He found his father crouched on the ground and moaning in pain. For some time even Alec had had the feeling that things were not working out so well on the property, but to a five-year-old things are not going to get any worse. Seeing his father slumped on the ground, though, he suddenly realised that perhaps they might.

In earlier days, before the floods of 1904, life at 'Shaftsbury' was all that the Griffiths family could have wished it to be. Bringing up his six children — Hilda, Vera, Una, Fred, Lock and Alec — at the small property 'Wollondale', on the shady banks of the Wollondilly near Towrang, had been trying for William, but he had seen an opportunity just out of Cootamundra, about 125 miles westwards along the railway line. John Barnes, member of parliament for Gundagai, had been seeking someone to manage his property, 'Shaftsbury'. Griffiths had got the job and, although the place fell short of the serene beauty of 'Wollondale', he knew the cottage would prove more than adequate for his family's needs. The land itself was so much more verdant than 'Wollondale'. With their ox and donkey and a few other possessions, the family moved to 'Shaftsbury', a few miles out of Cootamundra on the Wallendbeen road. They loved their new home. Their favourite place at 'Shaftsbury' was in front of the huge fireplace in their cottage. There they would indulge in some of life's simpler pleasures. The Griffiths family had very few visitors to the cottage and just to sit or play on the hearth, with only each other and the glowing embers for company, was truly wonderful.

Two more children were born at 'Shaftsbury' — sister Stella and baby brother John. Stella survived for only six months. Yet despite the unhappiness that her death brought to the family, they had felt that fortune was still smiling on them.

As more extremes of weather struck, this feeling waned. Rainless weeks became months and 1902 had brought the worst — and longest — drought ever recorded in New South Wales. Then the drought-breaking weather of 1903 — the weather the Griffiths family had so longed for — worsened. Windstorms (which the locals called a cyclone) lashed the property one night, and the next day the tearful children had watched their father forlornly surveying the shattered wheat fields. The wheat had been ready for harvest; hired hands had arrived just the previous day to help bring it in. The night after the windstorms, 'Shaftsbury' was hit by dreadful hail. Stones the size of small mangoes smashed every window in the homestead and the Griffiths cottage, destroyed much of the orchard including the ripened cherries that were to be picked the following day, and killed the laying hens and broke all the eggs.

In two nights, the life that William Griffiths had toiled over the years to build was destroyed. There was no money to replace the broken windows and the family was exposed to the elements for weeks. By the time the floods hit in 1904, the children felt sure that their father's heart was broken.

Now, standing beside his sister staring down the track, it seemed to Alec that his father had more than just a broken heart.

'Is Daddy sick, Hilda?'

'Yes, Alec. Daddy's sick', she said, wiping her eyes.

After Easter, William's health had become much worse. He had been in such pain recently that he seldom left his bed. Joining the family in their torment was William's old red cattle dog, who sensed his master's pain and lay curled up, whining constantly, under the bed. He seemed to sense the worst.

It was now late May and William was being admitted to the

small hospital in Cootamundra, up on the hill overlooking the cemetery. Only after several weeks did the doctor decide to operate, but there was no anaesthetic to be found. On 23 June 1905 — the day before a supply of anaesthetic arrived on the mail train from Sydney — William Griffiths died of liver disease. He was 46 years old. He was laid to rest in the cemetery, and his baby daughter Stella was taken up from her resting place and buried there next to him. A wooden cross was placed on the grave. Eliza Jane Griffiths could afford no more.

The Griffiths' prospects for wealth had only ever been meagre at best, but now were even less. No questions were asked in this land and help was only given if asked for. With seven children on her hands and no source of income, Eliza Jane wired her mother in Grafton. Could she bring the family to live with her? Grafton was the place of her birth, and the place where she had met William. Perhaps in Grafton she could start again.

There was no welfare to assist the likes of Eliza Jane Griffiths and family. They sold everything, right down to the pots and the pan — even their pillows. Friends from Cootamundra escorted them and their handful of possessions up to the railway station. To the south-west, an unrelieved black cloud menaced the distant hilltop and threatened storms. In a few weeks the Cootamundra wattle would start to bloom again. But none of this mattered now. In around eleven hours the Griffithses would be in Sydney. Alec, who had watched the trains steam by out the front of the 'Shaftsbury' property and had tried unsuccessfully to picture their faraway destinations, was eager to see a city. He had never seen one before.

* * *

There was a progressive atmosphere in Sydney that spoke of wide horizons and a burgeoning century. The mass of people, conspicuous only in their inconspicuousness, were friendly. The cobbled sunlit streets smiled. The family made their way down to the harbour, to the North Coast Steam Navigation Company wharf. In the slanting light of the winter sun the harbour looked surreal, beautiful beyond words. Pleasure boats jostled with ships for right of way, and hordes of seagulls followed in their wake searching for food. A breeze funnelled down the harbour, ensuring that the eternally hungry scavengers had to dance for their dinner. For the first time in his life — a life that begun unceremoniously at 'Wollondale' in the early hours of New Year's Day 1900 — the auburn-haired, cheekily grinning Hugh Alexander Waters Griffiths looked at seagulls and smiled at their comical shrieks. He gazed up at the enormous bridge of the SS *Kyogle* lying there with steam up for the passage north along the coast, and felt like the smallest person on earth. The *Kyogle* was not exactly a large ship but it was, after all, the first he had ever laid eyes on. And it was afloat in the first sea he had ever seen.

The Griffiths family were conducted aboard by one of the crew. Looking like a figure from a Cézanne painting, the unshaven man sucked thoughtfully on a pipe, his eyes seldom lifting from the wet deck. But such a courteous man for such an expressionless face! He gave every assistance to Eliza Jane, who was struggling with her seven children and the baggage. In a lamplit cabin well below decks he sold them one-way tickets for the northward passage, then disappeared into the bowels of the ship.

The children surfaced on deck again and leaned on the railing as they watched the people on the quay below watching *them* — many of them wharf idlers, who seemed to congregate lazily just to watch ships embarking on their voyages. Sydney was that kind of place, where even the busiest people seemed to be relaxing. There was an unhurried sense of well-being that could only have come from the knowledge that the city lay thousands of miles away from the rest of the European world. No one knew that feeling better than the horse-cab drivers who hovered around the quay and who soon became specks of black and grey as the narrow, iridescent strip of churned-up water behind the *Kyogle* widened and became smooth.

The seagulls left them as they steamed out through the Heads on what would be for the most part a calm passage. Young Alec felt a tremendous sadness at leaving behind his new love, Sydney Harbour. He vowed to return one day to see it again.

CHAPTER TWO
Fry Street

The seaspray haze of coastline, reaching ahead to infinity, guided the *Kyogle* northwards. Braving the spray on deck, Alec stood by the foremast with his brother Lock and searched for the first glimpse of the mouth of the Clarence. Brief interludes of mist-like rain broke through the now pewter-coloured sky as the ship moved up the wide river.

Derricks on the wharf waited to unload cargo ships that would no longer dock there — the railways were seeing to that. Shadowy figures moved about the wharf, waiting for the *Kyogle* to disgorge its complement of loved ones. Few of the Griffiths children had ever seen Granny. Nonetheless, they all found themselves peering over the railing, trying to pick out her wizened face among the crowd. It was some time before the passengers disembarked, and the waiting was making Alec restless. All that could be heard was the slap of water against the ship's hull, the creak of the wharf's pylons, and the murmur of an expectant crowd.

The Griffithses' new life began the moment they moved into Granny's old cottage in Fry Street. Typical of other cottages in the district, it was small and nondescript and of weatherboard construction. Sheets of rust-coloured bullnosed iron gave the roof some semblance of character. Out the back somewhere, a dog barked.

Granny was not at all well off and it proved difficult trying to accommodate so many people in a cottage built for two. With lifted brow, Granny pulled a chair away from the wicker table and sat down. Yes, her daughter had been through a tremendous ordeal in losing her husband. Yes, she would help her daughter as much as she could, but the kids would have to help out too. The next year would not be easy for any of the Griffiths family. Even at the age of five, that much was very clear to Alec.

By the middle of 1906, a year after her father's death, Hilda had not long to go at school until she turned fourteen, whereupon she would earn her own living through a variety of jobs working for local storekeepers. There was little else for her to do in Grafton. Before she left, Hilda saw to it that the rest of the kids were fully adapted to their new school and that they could cope without her being there. She also saw to it that they never dallied on the way home from school, for there was plenty of work to be done.

Vera picked up odd jobs here and there, while Una cleaned the cottage and cooked for her brothers outside school hours. In between these chores she picked fruit and vegetables for various people in the district, and was given fresh produce in return for her labours. Eliza Jane turned the front verandah into a small shop, where passers-by could purchase such items as biscuits, wicks and pouches of tobacco. The verandah looked like the home of a satin bowerbird that had collected all the bottletops and shiny objects this side of the Queensland border. Eliza Jane sold almost everything that couldn't be nailed down.

Like his brothers and sisters, Alec had to get work while at school to help make ends meet at the cottage. Coming home from school he dropped in at the local butcher's shop a few days a week. The butcher had no running water supply or electricity but he did have a well, and water had to be pumped up into an elevated storage tank. Thereafter it could be tapped using gravity. Alec had the job of pumping the water out of the well and up into the tank. The whole operation had to be done by hand, and depending on how empty the tank was at the time, it could take quite a while. No matter how many hours young Alec worked, his remuneration consisted of one bundle of sausages. Simple as that. Half an hour's work: a bundle of sausages. Three hours work: a bundle of sausages. In either event, the sausages were always very much appreciated at home.

One of Alec's earliest part-time jobs was for Tom J., a Salvation Army man who owned a fruit and vegetable shop in Grafton. Tom had a big patch of watermelons, of which he was especially proud. There came a time when he noticed that some of the melons were being stolen. Tom reckoned the thief was pretty good at what he did, because he only ever took the ripe ones, and only on the one night each week when Tom went into town. Tom had an idea that it had to be one of the locals who was pinching the melons, so he set a trap.

One evening, after the last of the cockatoos had concluded their raucous dusk symphony, Tom dropped in on the Griffiths household. He had a proposition for Fred. And Fred had a proposition for his younger brother Alec.

Tom J. would deliberately go past this bloke's place later that night so that the man could see him riding into town. This would be the lure for the thief to visit Tom's melon patch. Darkness came quickly to the Clarence district, and Grafton was not yet a large enough town for its lights to make a difference. A thick mist had blotted out most of the moon, but there was just enough light to ensure the success of the ruse. Anyway, the thief would surely know that the telltale clip-clop of hooves on the track could belong to no other horse than the one drawing Tom's sulky.

'Right, fellers,' Tom began, addressing Alec and his older brother Fred. Tom was smiling knowingly. It was less the smile of the cat that stole the cream than the smile of the man who was about to catch the cat. 'How about you two hide in the corn growing alongside the melons. Then when you see 'im ... well, you'll know what to do.'

'Sure thing, Mr J., you can count on us,' Fred replied. Tom left and the boys made their way to the melon patch.

An hour later, through the night's murkiness, the boys could just make out the man climbing through the fence, and wading through the waves of corn towards the melon patch. The next thing they knew, the fellow was pressing all the watermelons to see which ones were ripe. After he had pulled out a couple of melons, Fred sang out, 'Mr J.! Here's our man!'

But the thief must have known that Tom was still in town. Instead of fleeing, which the boys had thought he'd do, he went after them. Alec had never run faster in his life. Their bare feet trod the lumpy earth of a freshly ploughed field, and after dropping 'his' melons the thief picked up some clods of earth and started pelting Alec and Fred with them. He hit Alec square in the back with his second throw. All that that did was to make Alec run faster. Eventually youth triumphed over middle age and the boys got away.

They ran into Tom on his way back from town. 'Mr J., Mr J.,' cried Fred. 'We know who's pinchin' yer melons.' And so, on the basis of the boys' information, Tom J. had a summons served on the thief. Fred and Alec were to go to court as witnesses. Both boys were pretty keen on this, as it would mean a day away from school. That day soon came and, outside the courthouse, Tom leaned over towards Alec and whispered, 'Well now, Alec, if you don't cry in the court, I'll buy you an ice-cream.' Alec did cry — but only a little — and he didn't get his ice-cream. But he reckoned he deserved one, just for lying down in a freezing cold corn patch at night. And for enduring the pain and humiliation of the rock-hard clod of earth he'd copped in the back. Alec didn't have the courage to complain, but Fred seemed to sense his unhappiness. On the way home he put his hand on his little brother's shoulder and said, 'Never mind. I'll get you an ice-cream. I promise.'

Weeks passed without any sign of the reward. Just as Alec was beginning to think that Fred had forgotten his pledge, he forgot it himself when they got another job from Tom J. It was a weekend job and meant driving a horse-drawn cart loaded to the brim with watermelons. Their task was to sell them door to door or on the street. 'Watermelons! Watermelons!' they sang out at the top of their young voices, all the way down each street. A lot of the people who came out of their houses actually did so to tell the Griffiths boys to shut up, but usually they'd end up buying one or two. The plump, ripe melons varied in price, between tuppence and sixpence. The price was scratched into the skin of each melon. Ever the entrepreneur, Fred soon acquired the knack of altering the figure. The easiest change was making a '2d' into '3d'. Fred and Alec both reckoned that a commission of one penny was not half bad.

While Alec felt that justice of a sort had been done, he was more than a little conscience-stricken. But Fred insisted that they had been nothing more than middle men in a business deal, and as Fred was older than he was it was easy for Alec to regard Fred as the instigator.

That wasn't the last the two brothers had to do with Tom J. On a spring morning in 1909 one of the local dairy farmers woke up to find five of his best cows lying dead in a paddock. Tempted by the young lucerne in the adjoining paddock, they'd broken through the fence during the night and had had a huge feed, and then fatally bloated themselves by drinking a lot of water. Had it happened during the waking hours, the farmer could have saved them by plunging a knife into their stomachs to release the accumulated gas. This was often done in the Clarence district, provided the cows were caught in time.

Tom J. organised a working-bee to dispose of the dead animals before they became a problem. Alec reckoned that every farmer from the entire Clarence district showed up, not to mention some hangers-on like Fred and him. The men started by skinning the cows and then cutting off the legs. The carcasses were burned. After the work was done, beer flowed like cream in a butter factory. By the end of the day most of the farmers were pretty drunk, especially Tom.

The farmers wanted to divide up the dead cows' legs among themselves, to be used for dog and pig feed. 'I reckon I desherve a coupla exshtra legs, coz I was the one who organizshed id all,' Tom said, with remarkable clarity in the circumstances, adamant that he should get the lion's share.

'Okay, Tom, we'll give ya four,' chorused a few of the men. They put four legs in the bottom of Tom's dray and threw him in on top of them. Fred and Alec drove the cart home to Tom's place, but he was too heavy to lift out and too inebriated to be coaxed out. So they just unhitched the horse from the dray, threw a hessian bag over Tom and left him to sleep it off, with only his four cow's legs for company. The boys didn't get any more jobs from Tom after that night.

Theirs was a fairly big school in Grafton. Not too big, of course, but big enough to guarantee a sort of 'impersonality', unlike the schools in Towrang and Cootamundra. The kids had to walk three miles into school every day. The days would often begin with a frost or a fog — 'Welsh in character', their father would have said — but by the time they got to school the day had usually become fine enough to enjoy. The Griffiths children got off school at about three-thirty in the afternoon, but since they had a long walk home the teacher would let them out early if there was a storm approaching.

There were no motor vehicles to speak of in Grafton. Alec's feet were all he had to get him to and from school. All the traffic he saw on the streets was horse-drawn. The favourite mode of transport was the horse and sulky, the only protection from the weather being a blanket. Grafton's streets — all unmetalled — were fenced off, and lit only at crossroads by a kerosene lantern atop a post in the very centre of the intersection. Around each lamp post were four smaller posts to protect the lamp from carts lurching by. Alec reckoned a horse and cart would have to be going like the blazes to damage one of them. Every afternoon, the lamplighter would come along and light the lamps, bathing each fog-blanketed crossroads in a surreal light. Peculiarly comforting, it was a glow that Alec quickly grew to love. Yet it reminded him of somewhere he had never been. Crisp mornings saw the lamplighter extinguishing the lamps and trimming the wicks ready for lighting again in the afternoon. Occasionally the Griffiths children would chance upon the lamplighter and sing out 'Hello' as they walked home from school. A smile was always returned. Coming upon him as they did brightened their day, and they were even happier to get home to find their mother waiting for them.

The Fry Street cottage was bereft not only of electricity, gas and sewerage but of running water as well. All the water they used was drawn from an underground well, hauled up in a bucket on the end of a rope by means of a windlass. There was no bath in the cottage, let alone a bathroom. Washing and bathing were done in the big washtub and it was Alec's job to light a fire in the backyard, draw some water out of the well, heat it and then transfer it to the tub. At least when Eliza Jane made a pot of tea, the amount of water was small enough to be boiled directly in the kettle on the wood-fired stove. To economise on firewood the kids would get a cup of tea only when dinner was being cooked, or when Eliza Jane was doing the ironing. She loathed ironing, as the iron was so heavy that her arm grew weary with each garment. The children liked ironing time, since it meant that the stove had to be lit in order to heat the iron. And that meant a nice hot cup of tea.

Apart from the stove there was no heating and light came from a candle. A solitary kerosene lamp in the middle of the kitchen table was quite a luxury, when Granny allowed it to be lit, and it changed the atmosphere of the room to one of warm congeniality. This usually occurred when the Griffiths household played host to a card night. Euchre was popular among the adults, but the kids usually had to go to bed early. Most of them had to get up for early-morning chores before they set off for school.

The 'lavatory' outside the cottage consisted of a hole in the ground with a little shed built over the top. Inside was a small chair to sit on. That was the extent of it. It was often a bit on the nose, but thankfully it was well down the backyard. The family certainly knew about it if they had to get up in the middle of the night and venture out there, especially in winter. And the redback spiders, who always seemed to know when anyone was coming, had to be dissuaded from their aggressive intent with the burning wick of a candle.

Despite the little hardships life at Fry Street was never miserable. The Griffiths children never had any money to spend on entertainment and outings, but they were always able to keep themselves occupied. Now and then a stray fowl would wander into their backyard, never to walk out again. There was the challenge of catching the fowl and the delight in preparing it for dinner and actually eating it. To eat chicken was the utmost in luxury.

The kids' main pastime was swimming in the Clarence River. Their favourite bogey hole — frequented even if the weather dealt out a storm or two — was down at the sawmill's log yard. The yard ran right down to the edge of the riverbank; it was from there that all the timber was loaded onto sailing ships. After an invigorating swim the boys would lie on the bank, drunk on the aroma of freshly sawn logs, watching the 'show' seemingly performed just for their benefit by the timber yard workers and the ships' deckhands.

The sailing ships possessed no heavy lifting gear, so each one had a large rectangular porthole in the hull, for'ard on the starboard side just above the waterline. One by one the logs were floated out to the ship, lined up, and drawn through the porthole into the cargo hold with the assistance of a steam donkey engine and a winch mounted on deck. The hardwood logs that wouldn't float were taken over to the ships by barge, and drawn through in the same way. Sometimes the barges took quite a while to reach the ships; this happened when the Griffiths boys commandeered the occasional barge to use as a diving platform, and got in the way.

Fred, Alec and their middle brother Lock became pretty friendly with most of the ships' crews during these early years in Grafton. The men seemed to be as entertained by the boys' antics in the water as the boys were by the men's work. Every now and again the captain of one of the ships of the Craig line, and a few of his crew, came to visit the boys at home, and to have a singsong around

Granny's old beaten-up piano. In return, they'd row the boys up the Clarence in the ship's overladen longboat — with barely two inches of freeboard to spare — for a Sunday picnic on the riverbank. Another crew the boys saw a lot of came from the *Mary Isabel.* The captain, a man named Walter, would often bring some of his men to visit the Griffiths sisters — as potential suitors, one would surmise. Vera was very keen on the second mate, Harry McN. — was in love with him, if truth be told — but nothing was to come of it. In 1910, when Eliza Jane took ill and the children were convinced that she was going to die, Alec overheard Hilda confiding in Walter that she was terrified of what would happen to the family 'if Mother were to join Father'. Walter's answer was simply to propose marriage.

Eliza Jane recovered. Hilda did not marry Walter. Nonetheless, the potential suitors continued to drift in. And Fred continued to let off bungers behind the settee whenever one of them sat down with one of his sisters.

CHAPTER THREE
Up Clarence Way

There's a trade you all know well -
It's bringing cattle over -
I'll tell you all about the time
When I became a drover.
I made up my mind to try the spec,
To the Clarence I did wander,
And brought a mob of duffers there
To begin as an overlander.

Anon. 'The Overlander'

The year 1910 was also when Alec started to work for his Uncle Charlie. During the school holidays he would go bush with him and help him out. Uncle Charlie owned a tip dray and two horses, and not much else. The most interesting time for Alec happened when Charlie was working as an ore contractor and they did a round trip up to a mine on the upper Clarence up past Baryulgil, then back down to Copmanhurst. The distance was less than 100 miles but the journey took almost a month. Roads were nonexistent, and frequently they had to clear thick scrub away in order to get to their destination for the night. They lived mostly on damper, though occasionally they shot kangaroos with Charlie's muzzle-loader.

The bush, Alec soon learned, had a special lure all of its own. Work was hard. Pleasures were few. Nonetheless he found himself immersed in the sounds, sights and smells of his surroundings, and loved it. Before long he understood why the shearers, squatters, rouseabouts and cockies lived the life they did. And why people like his Uncle Charlie — men who were gunmen 'on the wallaby', but songmen around a fire — never wanted that life to change.

As Charlie worked hard, the word had got around. It wasn't long before he got a contract with the local council to take wooden girders to bridge sites north of Grafton. The council was building a road heading up north, parallel to the railway but a mile or two away, and the road had to cross over several creeks. Wooden girders for the bridges were prepared in the sawmill in Grafton, and then taken out by rail and dropped by the side of the line at the closest point to where each bridge was to be built. It was Charlie's job to pick up the girders and haul them with his tip dray through the dense scrub to each bridge site.

With a homemade windlass he'd lift one end of a girder onto the back of the dray and make it fast. Then, with one horse in the shafts and the other one out in front, he and Alec would set off, dragging the girder through the scrub. There weren't any tracks, let alone roads, and so for the first trip at each spot the pair had to hack their way through. Every fold in the ground seemed like a mountain to be conquered. There were quite a few girders for each bridge, and although it might be only a mile or so away from the railway line it often took them four or five days to haul the beams to the site. Alec must have been helpful to Charlie — or perhaps just a good companion — because he always took him along.

The days were sweltering; the sort of days best suited for sitting on a cool, shaded verandah drinking beer or lemonade. But the sun-baked scrub and the task at hand didn't allow for such luxuries. Relaxation came only at dusk, when Alec and Charlie would camp beside a creek, where there was plenty of fresh water for the horses.

At the end of each day's work it was Alec's job to collect wood, light a fire to boil the billy, and prepare the evening meal. With no ice for refrigeration their selection of food was a bit limited. But they survived perfectly well enough on a few saveloys, potatoes, bread and treacle, dripping, eggs and flour. When the bread got stale a few days into the trip — and if there was time before darkness fell — Alec would mix up some flour and make a damper in the hot ashes of the fire.

Charlie was usually pretty busy in the evening while Alec prepared the food. After unharnessing the horses, watering them and feeding them, he'd fit the hobbles. These consisted of a loose chain fastened from one front leg to the other, and meant you didn't have to tether the horses. They never wandered too far from the camp.

The darkness was always welcome, for it brought with it the coolness so longed for during the heat of the day. It also brought with it mosquitoes the size of a cart, but Alec and Charlie could do little about them except stay close to the smoke of the fire. After cooking the damper Alec would spread the swags out on the ground beneath the dray. Before they put their heads down they'd sit by the coals and talk in between and sometimes during mouthfuls of delicious damper. Charlie never said much but what he did say, Alec reckoned, was worth listening to.

'Nothing wrong with an honest day's work,' he'd say, staring into the scrub. 'I reckon it's the best thing a bloke can do.'

The dying fire after a hard day's work was the surest sleeping pill. Curled up underneath the dray, Alec would listen to the sounds of the bush. He was never more content than when he could drift off to sleep to the sound of raindrops falling on the floor of the dray just above him. The sound of animals in the scrub — only just waking up from *their* sleep — was strangely comforting too. He was well fed, warm and dry. And he was happy. Life up in the bush was pretty good.

* * *

Summer was also the time for swimming. A quarter of a mile or so down the Clarence from a farmer's house near Grafton was a beaut swimming hole. Midstream, an uninhabited island was fragrant with the aroma of adventure. The current flowed swiftly and strongly in the middle of the river, and gently at the banks. There were no rapids here because the water was too deep at this point. The entire river held great allure for Alec and his brothers; it was the highway to the world beyond and one day, the boys knew, they would follow it. But for the moment the river was simply a friend, like the summer breezes off the water that helped cool the boys in the oppressive summer heat. What more could one want? Who would not choose to heed the sound of flowing water on such hot days? Certainly not the Griffiths boys. They lived for these days; days of clear blue skies and quiet swimming holes. Minutes would pass as though they were hours. Numerous wild ducks, and the half-wild ducks that the farmer kept, often paddled over to the island to lay their eggs. The farmer had given the boys permission to eat as many eggs as they could get their hands on, so long as they didn't take any away. Many a day they'd grab a jam tin from home, a box of matches, some salt, and if they were lucky some bread and butter — more often than not they had to content themselves with bread and dripping. To get butter was rare, especially in the searing, flyblown heat of a northern New South Wales summer. Butter was sold in 'butterboats' made out of thin sheets of wood, about eight inches square, and folded up at each end to form a (supposedly) leak-proof container. On the rare occasions that the Griffiths household could afford to buy butter, by the time they got it home it was not just watery but a mass grave for flies. The only 'refrigeration' they had consisted of a perforated iron cage covered by a wet bag around the outside. Every day one of the kids was given the job of keeping the bag wet.

Down on the riverbank the boys would strip off all their clothes and swim naked across to their island. Lock often tried to go most of the way underwater; the only evidence of his passage a moving 'V' of ripples through the eddies and the whirlpools. The current was strong, but there were duck eggs to be had! Fred had the hardest job in this tricky manoeuvre — he was the eldest, after all. He had to swim using one arm only, as his other arm was holding the tin above the water to keep the boys' precious matches dry.

On the island they'd fill the tin with water and light a fire. It was quite a sight from the riverbank, three stark-naked lads racing around in broad daylight, shooing away the occasional duck and gathering eggs. If they found a nest with a lot of eggs in it they didn't take any, as the boys reckoned it must have been a fair while since they'd been laid. The sight of a new family of ducklings swimming alongside them in the river was always enough to deter them from taking eggs from any of these nests. And so they'd raid only the nests with a few eggs in them. After boiling the eggs they ate them on the spot. They had to be cooked really hard so that the boys could eat them without a spoon.

The only problem with these escapades was that often the boys would get back to the calm waters just off the riverbank and find a few of the local girls watching them, giggling, from among the trees. This wouldn't have been a real drama if the girls hadn't always hidden the boys' clothes.

* * *

Just before he turned eleven, Alec was given work on a nearby dairy farm. A few times each week he went there and helped out with the cows. Eventually he learned how to milk them. In return, the farmer gave him a large billycan of milk for every five or six cows he milked. With extra work such as this to try and help balance the family budget, there wasn't a lot of spare time for 'entertainments' during the week, so he and his brothers made their own fun on the way to school.

The route crossed many paddocks full of grass tussocks. A handful of hares called the paddocks home, and the boys knew they simply curled up in the lumps of grass rather than building a burrow. It didn't take long for the lads to grow wise to the particular tussocks in which the hares lived. Sometimes they'd manage to catch them. Pretending to be hunters, they'd stalk stealthily over to a tussock, sneak up behind the hare and grab him by the back legs. They never hurt him — just grabbed his hind legs and walked him the few miles to school like a wheelbarrow. Once they got to school they'd let him go, unharmed but well exercised.

On the weekends they'd often go to one or another of the neighbouring farms, borrow a couple of horses — a very quiet one for Alec — and go for a ride. Fred was now a top rider and frequented many of the surrounding properties, breaking in their horses in exchange for a loan of them. One day he said to Alec, 'How'd ya like to come and help me work a horse in?' Although Alec was still learning to ride at this stage, he agreed, trying to conceal his fear but wanting to earn his older brother's respect.

Out at the property, Fred took a young horse. For Alec he selected the youngster's dam. Slowly, at first, the two boys rode off into the bush. 'We gotta go for a gallop,' Fred suddenly called out and, before Alec could even think of protesting, Fred disappeared at breakneck speed. 'Mother' wanted to follow her youngster and took off in hot pursuit. After a few surprised moments, Alec fell from the mare's back and found himself in a situation that terrifies any horse rider.

He was not completely off. He was almost off, except for his left foot, which was caught in the stirrup. Fortunately Alec had fallen to the right. Somehow he prevented his head being banged along on the rocky ground. Unfortunately, in doing this, his hands bounced and scraped on the ground for a good two hundred yards before 'Mother' had mercy on him and came to a sudden halt.

Fred came back, and laughed. 'How about getting me down?' pleaded Alec. Before Fred extricated his younger brother he laughed again. 'That looked absolutely bonzer!' he exclaimed. Alec, whose hands were raw, didn't share his brother's enthusiasm. At least the only bruising was to Alec's pride. After that day, Alec became a very good rider very quickly.

Alec's newfound ability came in handy a couple of months later. Whenever one of the local cattlemen was planning a muster, one of the cockies would be given the task of enlisting all the help he could from anyone in the district who was a half-decent rider. Never mind how old the riders were, so long as they could ride. Often the cattle that had to be mustered had been out bush for up to twelve months without seeing either humans or horses. And there'd be a lot of new calves in the mob that had never laid eyes on either. The potential for breakaways during a muster was significant. The cattleman would therefore take only the best riders out front with him. The rest would hang back, as 'spares'. Before too long, young Alec became a pretty good 'spare'. The horses were pretty good too. They knew exactly what to do if a beast broke away from the mob. As soon as a horse saw a cow or a steer try to break away, it'd be off like the blazes after it. The 'spares' like Alec didn't have to do anything except stay on. But they had to be good riders to stay on, as the horses usually tore off without warning and most of the riders rode bareback.

By the time he went out on muster up front for the first time, Alec was so accustomed to riding horses that he rode bareback too. His horse was jumping around all over the place, but the jeers he'd get from other men on the muster if he came a cropper were a greater incentive to stay on than the prospect of a thoroughly bruised backside.

When they'd eventually get the cattle back to the yard, the beasts that had never been seen before had to be branded. The ringers would catch a calf and tie its legs, and the station owner would get hold a long iron bar with his brand — usually his own initials — on the flat end of it. Alec, whose job was to light the fire to heat the end of the bar, didn't like watching when the brand was burned into the animal's hide. But the men reckoned it was the only way of doing it since the brand would remain for the whole life of the beast. And when they told Alec it didn't hurt, mustering became another weekend sport for him. It was on one of these musters that he smoked his first cigarette, made of dried cow dung wrapped in brown paper. It was also his last.

Like many other regional towns in Australia, Grafton was still full of 'new century' hopes. The promise of prosperity hung so thick in the air you could almost smell it. The present, in the guise of a burgeoning railway and transport network, was exciting. Yet the past, in the shape of the tall sailing ships that sailed up the Clarence, was somehow serene and comforting. It refused to die.

A railway line ran northwards though a line was yet to run to Sydney. There was no road transport to speak of either, which left you with the North Coast Steam Navigation Company or the immortal sailing ships that took sawlogs down to Sydney. Running steamers like the *Kalatina* and the *Kyogle*, the company had the produce transport game pretty much sewn up.

In the town itself, horse and cart traffic across the mighty Clarence was catered for by one small punt. Foot passengers were ferried back and forth across the river by the *Helen*. A handful of other steamers — the *Clarence*, the *Woolwich*, the *Lady Beatrice* and the *Iolanthe* — plied the Clarence River as traders, collecting dairy produce and cream cans from properties along the riverbank. Very shallow water was the domain of a drogher. This was little more than a punt, but had an enormous paddlewheel. To Alec, the paddlewheel was gargantuan. He could not imagine anything heavier on earth. Every time he saw the drogher he was convinced that its front would lift out of the water and that it would sink, paddlewheel first, to the bottom of the Clarence. He was also convinced that he should be there to see it when it happened, and followed the craft from his favourite points of vantage whenever he could. The drogher brought produce into Grafton — mainly bags of potatoes and corn and the like. It could get right up into the upper reaches of the Clarence, where the traders couldn't go. It was also a region where Alec had never really been and he often wondered how different the world must be, so far away from home.

The local storekeeper ran a large motor launch called the *Fair Trader*. Stocked up with almost everything the property owners and their families could ever need, he did a regular run up and down the river. If anyone wanted anything he didn't have on board, he'd carve the details into a plank of wood kept for just such a purpose, and bring the goods with him on his next trip. Business was, for the most part, conducted on a barter system. As payment for goods supplied, the storekeeper collected a heap of eggs and other farm produce. Lucky bloke, Alec often thought — living a life where money's irrelevant. The only thing the storekeeper ever had to worry about was keeping his eggs from breaking and ensuring he always had a piece of wood to 'write' on.

Life wasn't so charmed for the Griffiths family. Even with the option of bartering for things rather than paying for them, times got no easier. In addition to his other jobs Alec got seasonal work on a small orange orchard. It was his job to keep the ground clear by picking up the 'windfalls' — the oranges that had fallen off the trees. He wasn't paid for the work, but was allowed to take home as many oranges as he could carry in his shirt. These were very much appreciated, for his mother could not afford to buy them. Nor could she afford to buy tomatoes, so occasionally Alec would take a big bucket to another farm not far away, pay the farmer thruppence, and fill the bucket with beautiful tomatoes straight off the vines.

Despite his contributions, and all the efforts of Vera, Hilda, Una, Fred and Lock, it became increasingly difficult to make ends meet. Eliza Jane decided to look further afield to try and build a better life for the family. Granny had passed away a couple of years earlier, in 1909, and since then there had been little to keep Eliza Jane in Grafton. While she was devastated by the loss, grief was a luxury reserved for those who didn't have to fight to make a living. Alec had never seen anyone so sad. He was sad too, but was becoming tougher in the face of hardships which fate continually tried to deal his family. In the space of a few years Eliza Jane had lost her husband and her mother. Now, with seven children on her hands, she felt she had to make a new start in a bigger town.

In love with ships, she had been to Sydney in 1908 to see a flotilla of United States Navy vessels, and had fallen in love not so much with the ships as with Sydney. The stunning harbour called to her, as did the promise of a new life for her family. Yet in the end she made the decision to send Alec and Lock off to work on a big dairy farm at Lower Southgate, near a hamlet called Lawrence. She simply couldn't afford to keep the two boys any more. Nor could she afford at the time to pay for the voyage to Sydney for the rest of the family, and it would be another year before they would be able to head south.

CHAPTER FOUR
Two Brothers

Lawrence was on the Clarence River closer to the coast. It was way up bush, off the beaten track. The hundred wings of a flock of cockatoos flashed through the sky, and then all was quiet for a moment as they settled into the loftiest gums. Suddenly, in raucous dissonance, they screeched a welcome to Lock and Alec. Below them, a side stream of the Clarence and sundry fern-matted creeks formed the boundaries between the paddocks, and the gilt-tinged fern fronds, waving in the breeze, joined the cockatoos in a welcoming dance.

With only each other and the possums in the rafters for company, the boys settled into their quarters in a small shack adjoining the homestead. The property was owned by two men in their twenties, assisted by the mother of one of them. It was run primarily to supply cream to the butter factory in Grafton, and ran about thirty cows. Work started the very next day. The brothers woke at four o'clock, rounded up the cows, drove them back to the yard where the milking bails were, and milked them. This was to be their daily lot from now on. There were no sheds, and if it was wet the raindrops seemed to have a mind of their own. They gathered on the cows' backs and then washed over Alec and Lock as they did the milking.

In wet weather the mud in the yards was at least a foot deep. During the winter, the brothers' job became quite an unpleasant one. It didn't help that the owners stayed in until the milking was done. Lock was now fourteen years old and Alec twelve. Alec had yet to get his first pair of shoes — he had never felt the ground with soles other than his own, or of borrowed shoes. When he walked barefoot on the frozen grass, the ice came up through his toes. Occasionally there was some comfort. Most of the cows would still be lying down when Alec arrived to herd them in, and when they knew he was there they got to their feet. After standing up the first thing they did was to empty their bowels. What a treat it was for Alec to plunge his feet into the hot, sloppy heaps! But he could not stand there very long. If he was late back to the yard with the cows, the owners would somehow find out and he could get into serious trouble and even lose his job.

The milking was always done by hand, after which the boys would put the milk through a separator, a machine turned by hand. The butter factory in Grafton was only interested in the cream, which went up the Clarence by boat. Lock and Alec used the separated milk to feed the pigs and dogs, and of course the calves. They would then wash all the buckets and cans, ready for the hours after school, when they'd have to milk the cows again. The following morning, after doing the milking once more and eating a spartan breakfast, they would get dressed to go to school and walk the three miles across the paddocks to get there. Theirs was a one-teacher school, situated on top of a steep hill. Alec and Lock weren't always there on time, but they reckoned that the teacher must have understood their position, for she was very lenient with them.

It wasn't too long before Alec came to know the habits of the hares in these paddocks too, and whenever he caught one he'd wheelbarrow it to school, just as he'd done in Grafton. He tried his best not to hurt the hares — after all, they were the main ingredient in the Hare Hunt, held every week at different farms. Every fourth weekend it was their turn.

On the morning of Alec and Lock's first Hare Hunt, the weather was warm but a cool breeze fanned their hair, and there was rain in the air that could be smelt but not seen or heard. The stockmen and dairy farmers from the surrounding districts, and some from even further afield, assembled at the farm on horseback. Heralding their arrival was the cracking of whips, and the barking of the cattle dogs and kangaroo dogs which accompanied the men. The Hare Hunt was a big event for the district and attracted quite a turnout, with all the men placing bets on their dogs' performance to see which one would come out the best. The wagers were seldom monetary. 'Two bales, Bill,' shouted one, chewing on a piece of bark. 'My best hobble-chains,' his friend countered.

All the ringers and hangers-on called their dogs and set off across the paddocks at a walking pace. They would camp on the property tonight, and the jingle of tinware blended in with the sound of their mounts' hooves striking stone. Somewhere in the grasses hares loitered, no doubt laughing at the 'rabbit-proof' fence they continually breached. One of the cattle dogs bounded off ahead, scouring the tussocks. Ears erect and with a drawn-out howl (of the type all the dogs seem to give when they first give chase) he set off after his quarry.

The hare has a secret weapon: the ability to change direction much more quickly than its foe can. But hares only ever do this at the last minute. And even without their favourite tactics — the double, the diagonal dash, the turn — a feinting hare is a tricky target. Yet the dog is faster and, Alec thought, much more beautiful to watch. Sadly, sometimes a dog would try to follow a hare through a fence and get so badly injured in the wire that it had to be destroyed.

The hare fleeing the cattle dog was joined by other hares. The dog was joined by other dogs. And the whole arena was filled with the dust of dodging hares, sprinting dogs and galloping horses. The hares were quick to take advantage of the many places they could beat the dogs to — low scrub, hollow logs or the nearby cane field. The dogs didn't catch any of the hares that day and in future Hare Hunts they seldom would. So it was finally decided that if there was no 'kill' the dog leading the pack when the hare turned — when it made that sudden, 90-degree or diagonal dash — would get the credit. But the owner would collect the winnings.

The Hare Hunt was just about the extent of the boys' spare-time activities. Any time not taken up in the dairy on the weekends was spent in the vegetable garden or slashing scotch thistles and blackberry bushes out in the paddocks. Sometimes the brothers would have to ride horses bareback and take the cows whose milk had dried up to the back paddock about six miles from the homestead. Then they'd bring back any of the cows that had new calves. Such jobs were quite a break from the monotony of milking cows. Alec enjoyed them immensely. But there was another job he loathed — a job nobody else would do. If a new calf was a heifer it was reared; eventually it would become a useful milking cow. But if it was a bull calf it had to be destroyed. First Alec had to kill the calf with a blow to its head using the blunt edge of an axe. He would then skin the animal with a sharp knife — a particularly gruesome task as it was necessary to skin it slowly and carefully. This was to ensure that he didn't cut any holes in the skin, which would lessen its value. He then had to lay the skin out on the ground and cover it with coarse salt, before rolling it up into a bundle and tying it with string. Finally he would carve up the calf's carcass into little pieces, boil them in a laundry copper over a fire in the open, and feed them to the dogs and pigs. Any leftovers would sit around for a while, producing an abominable stench.

The calf skins were traded for other goods with a travelling storekeeper who came to Lawrence once a week in a covered wagon drawn by two horses. The storekeeper supplied almost everything in exchange and accepted skins, poultry, eggs and other farm produce. He always brought a newspaper along with him. While he was trading goods with the owners of the property, Alec would secretly scan the paper. He wanted to see if the government was doing anything about child labour.

It wasn't. Boys like Alec and Lock continued to work very long hours for very little money. They never asked to play such a part in the new nation and nobody consulted them; it was just the way things worked out.

Besides milking and tending the cows, Alec was forever busy collecting eggs from the haystacks, from out in the scrub and from underneath unfriendly blackberry bushes since the hens ran free. Alec and Lock also had the job of pulling the corn when it was ripe. Once they'd pulled the cobs off the stalks they threw them into a 44-gallon drum, which was mounted on a sled drawn by a horse going up and down the rows. The corn was then stored in the barn and had to have the husks taken off by hand before the grain could be got off the cob. A more monotonous job could not have existed, Alec felt, but one day the farmers hit upon the cunning idea of holding a corn-husking competition. This was just fine with Lock and Alec. The competition was to be held at a different property each week. Each competitor was given a dozen husks of corn, which certainly helped to reduce the pile. For his work on the farm, Alec was paid half a crown — two shillings and sixpence — per week. He sent this to his mother to help keep food on the table. But despite this the time came for Eliza Jane to take the family south, where prospects were better. With some of the money from the sale of her mother's cottage she paid the fares for the voyage down to Gosford, after which they would make their way to her sister Bella's in Newcastle until a house became available in Sydney. Since Lock and Alec were self-supporting where they were, they were to be left behind. It was felt that they would be too much of a burden to their mother if they went south too.

Once a week the boat to Sydney left Grafton at night, calling in at Lawrence around midnight. The night the family left, Lock and Alec went into Lawrence to say goodbye to them. It was not a happy prospect for Alec.

Clouds raced in front of the moon as deckhands loaded the last of the ship's cargo. As Alec watched, restlessness overwhelmed him. Shortly, with the embarking of the last passengers, it was found that he was missing. The crew and Alec's family spent over an hour searching for him, to no avail. Disgruntled passengers decided they would prefer to sit out the delay on the wharf, and a number of them disembarked. Meanwhile, Alec had found himself a comfortable hiding place. It would be a long voyage, without food or water. At least he would rediscover the pleasure of more than a few hours of unarrested sleep. But why hadn't Lock joined him? What caged hare, given the chance to escape, would turn its back on an open hutch door?

The boat lurched first to starboard, then to port. The noise of the engine reached a crescendo, and Alec imagined the sound of hawsers, first pulled taut and then released, splashing into the water. He drifted off to sleep, smiling.

He awoke to the sight of a ruddy face, cloaked in a grey sailor beard, peering down at him. Never mind, it didn't matter now. The captain would ask some questions and then reunite him with his family. He had pulled it off! Then Alec realised that the engines had stopped. 'Sydney!' he exulted, as he was dragged up on deck.

But Sydney looked uncannily like Lawrence. And the angry faces that peered at him from the night's murkiness seemed frightfully familiar. The boat had never left the wharf, and there on the deck was his brother Lock. Lock too had tried to stow away, but being taller than Alec had been less successful in finding a snug hiding place. Unceremoniously, the two Griffiths boys were put back ashore, but not before being chided in public by their mother. With a sonorous blast of its horn, the ship pulled away from the wharf, two and a half hours late. Lock and Alec watched with sadness as the steamer — and their family — disappeared into the night.

On the three-mile walk back to the farm, the pair resolved to go to Sydney as soon as they possibly could. 'Alec,' Lock said, 'I found out from one of the fellers on the ship how much it is.'

'How much?' Alec was barely able to contain his excitement.

'Seventeen and six each. So with two and six a week each in wages, it'll take seven weeks to save our fare.'

And so it did. By the time seven weeks had passed they had saved enough to go home. Home! They had never seen it — they didn't even know where it was exactly — but they knew it was home because their family was there. On the night the boys knew the steamer would be calling in at Lawrence, they went to bed as usual but arose at eleven that night. and packed their belongings. This was an easy task, for everything Lock and Alec owned fitted into a flour bag. After placing pillows under the covers to make it look as though they were still there in bed, they departed. Sneaking out of the house they had few feelings of guilt or broken loyalty. After all, they weren't really running away from home. They were running to it.

Their final three-mile walk — or was it a gallop? — down to the river at Lawrence was a wondrous experience. They could smell freedom. Their legs and bare feet were soon cut and grazed from scampering over rocks and constantly falling over, but they didn't care. Perhaps they didn't even notice.

CHAPTER FIVE
The Harbour Town

Even though Alec had only seen Sydney once before, he felt as though he really was coming home. Was it that indescribable sense of warm welcome one feels on coming in through the Heads? Or was it the sun glistening on the serene harbour? He wasn't certain, but he could be sure of one thing. The reception he received on arriving at his mother's doorstep in Bridge Road, Glebe (having had a devil of a time finding her, with only a sender's address on a letter as a guide) was anything but warm.

For Lock it was different. He was now old enough to leave school and soon found work in the Post Office, and consequently was allowed to live in the Glebe house along with the rest of the family. Hilda and Vera had been successful in getting jobs as sales hands at Grace Brothers on Broadway, and Una had found work as a 'mother's help' in a doctor's home. Lock joined Fred as a Post Office telegraph messenger, while Jack was still a youngster at school. All the Griffiths children lived under the one roof.

Except for thirteen-year-old Alec. Too young to leave school, and not old enough anyway to get gainful employment in Sydney, he was packed off to yet another dairy farm, this time just outside Newcastle. There a shock awaited him. Instead of getting out of bed at four o'clock in the morning to milk the cows, he had to get up at midnight every day of the week as the milk had to be delivered to the Newcastle suburbs early each morning. Usually he would be able to get back to bed by about five, snatch a couple of hours' kip before breakfast, and then walk two miles to school in Mayfield. He was never paid any wages for his job, just fed. Fourteen was the school-leaving age and as that magic birthday — 1 January 1914 — approached he decided to give up school and leave the dairy farm. While the owners were reluctant to let him go, they gave him their blessing and generously paid his fare to Sydney.

It was fortunate that he was not expecting a 'welcome home' celebration at the house in Glebe, for he would have been disappointed. Alec's turning up, and the arrival of a young boarder by the name of Frank, brought the number of occupants in the house to nine. The terrace house had three small bedrooms and a backyard the size of a handkerchief. The rent paid by the boarder made things a little easier financially, so Eliza Jane decided that Alec could stay at home on condition that he find a job as soon as possible. In the meantime he would attend Forest Lodge School in Glebe.

* * *

At the beginning of August 1914, war broke out. Fred and Lock signed up almost immediately as wireless operators in the merchant navy. (Like other fourteen-year-old boys, Alec tried to enlist to go and fight for Australia in the Kaiser's war, but only succeeded in being laughed at by the enlistment officer.) The outbreak of hostilities required that all ships, regardless of whether or not they were men-of-war, be equipped with wireless. As wireless telephony was unheard of, the ships relied on wireless telegraphy. No trouble was encountered in procuring the Morse sets — it was men trained to operate them that were scarce. This shortage of wireless operators wasn't just confined to the Antipodes, either — it spread the length and breadth of the world. Wireless, like aviation, was very much a 'new science'.

Over the ensuing few months the Griffiths household heard little news of the Kaiser's war, except for HMAS *Sydney*'s magnificent triumph over the *Emden*. This news was soured only by scuttlebutt that the *Sydney*'s captain had got too close to the German ship and could in fact have sunk the *Emden* from a lot further away, without sustaining casualties. Nonetheless, for the first time the Griffiths family — like all Australians — felt that their nation had really entered the war. In December Fred became the wireless operator on the troopship A-37 *Barambah*. The *Barambah* was part of Convoy No. 2 of Australian and New Zealand troopships used to transport the men, horses and supplies of the 4th Australian Infantry Brigade off to Egypt. Soon Lock became the wireless operator on A-36 *Boonah*, part of the same convoy. It was a few weeks after his sixteenth birthday.

Later, a postcard from Lock and letters from Fred convinced Alec of the good time his brothers must be having. That's what I'm going to do, he thought to himself one evening after school — learn the Morse code and join the Navy. The prospects for adventure were irresistible and Alec didn't really think of the dangers. Few of the boys who enlisted did. To learn the Morse code properly you needed money, so Alec left school and went for a job at George Hudson's, the timber merchants down on Blackwattle Bay, and was successful. The timber that came in by ship was to be unloaded on the water and floated across to the mill. The logs were sawn into planks with a large bandsaw. As a junior clerk, it was Alec's job to go around the mill and give the men their instructions. This was a fairly monotonous job, but it meant money.

When he was not at work, Alec was busy falling in love with Sydney. Life there was a simple affair. Almost all the traffic was horse-drawn and the horses' hooves struck wood or stone as they trotted noisily on their way. Most of the streets were paved with wooden blocks about the size of a house brick. Alec became fascinated with the task of the road workers as they put down the new paving, dipping the wooden blocks in hot tar and then placing them in position on a concrete foundation with the wood grain running vertically. Such precision, for something as simple as a road. The number of horses on the streets was so great that not only did they wear out the wooden blocks quickly but their droppings created a major problem. The council had to employ young boys to continually patrol the streets, long-handled broom and shovel in hand, to sweep up the manure, which would then be deposited into steel boxes set into the kerbstones at regular intervals, to be collected later by lorry. The lads were nicknamed 'sparrow-starvers' and received little money and even less thanks — especially from the sparrows.

Home life in Sydney was also a simple affair. Most houses had a fuel stove in the kitchen, which was used both for cooking and for heating the house. The more affluent people had a gadget on their stove which served more or less as a hot water system. In addition, many houses had a coal fire in the lounge room or very occasionally in the main bedroom.

The bulk of Sydney's coal came from Newcastle on colliers. These ships would steam in through the Heads and down the harbour past Pyrmont. Sometimes while working at Hudson's timber yard Alec watched them moor at the wharf at the head of Blackwattle Bay, against Bridge Road. The coal had to be unloaded from the colliers into a large bin on the wharf. In doing this, the wharfies put on a veritable circus act.

First they erected a plank about forty feet in the air, with one end resting on top of the coal bin and the other supported over the ship's hold by ropes. The wharfies then took a rope with a hook on its end from the ship's winch up through a pulley block, suspended about thirty feet above the plank, and down to the bottom of the ship's hold. This rope was then hooked onto a basket which had already been filled with coal, one shovel-load at a time. One bloke did a balancing act on the end of the plank suspended above the hold. 'Ready on!' the overseer would sing out, and the winch would start to raise the basket to the height of the plank. The balancing man would guide the basket over to the bin where the coal was tipped. As the winch was reversed, he would go into the tightrope routine of his act and walk smartly back along the narrow plank, whereupon he would guide the now empty basket back into the ship's hold. From the wharf the coal was delivered in steam-driven wagons with solid rubber tyres to customers all over Sydney town. With his older brothers off at the war, Alec had become something of a loner. The wharfside entertainment was a chance to defeat boredom.

At Hudson's one day, Alec's boss strode up to him, looking purposeful. 'Griffiths!' he boomed, 'jump on a bicycle right away and race over to the *Herald* office and grab a paper.' Alec didn't know what his boss had heard, but what he'd heard had clearly made a tremendous impact.

Although unused to bicycles, Alec raced over to the office of the *Sydney Morning Herald* and got a copy hot off the press, literally. The paper was still warm to the touch, but Alec had no time to check if the ink was dry. His boss had ordered him to race, so race he did. He paid for the paper, shoved it down his shirt, and took off back to Hudson's timber yard. Most of the workers couldn't read, so the boss read from the paper aloud. The men could scarcely contain their excitement when they heard the news. Australians had landed in the Dardanelles! The workers' chests swelled with pride, especially Alec's. His brothers must surely have been on the troopships that took them there. After that day, Alec rode over to the *Herald* office every time his boss heard — or imagined he'd heard — that there was something doing in what had by now become known simply as 'the European war'.

Alec was still far too young to join up, so he decided to spend his evenings learning the Morse code. The boarder Frank joined him. Sharing a room with Frank worked in well with Alec's plans. In order to learn Morse code telegraphy there had to be two people: one to send the message, and one to receive it. The Morse equipment consisted of just a couple of pieces of brass and a buzzer, but it did the job. The pair hadn't been practising all that long when they decided to enrol at the new Marconi Telefunken Wireless School in York Street. Alec used most of his wages to pay his fees. The whole arrangement at the school was fairly primitive, and the course itself had the air of being a rushed job — as a direct consequence of the shortage of wireless operators for the war.

The school had brought an instructor in off a ship. Ghostlike, he appeared in front of the class on the first day, and said, 'I apologise for the fact that I am unable to instruct the class. I have been brought here at short notice from a ship, and have never instructed before.' Looking hesitant, he then added phlegmatically, 'Besides, I have no instructional books here with me.'

As he turned on his heel to leave, a book was thrust into his hand by someone in the front row. For a fleeting moment a look of incredulity swept across his face, to be replaced by the resigned look of a man who's just been dobbed in to make a speech at the wedding of a distant acquaintance. He began instructing the class.

It was the beginning of a long and arduous road towards enlistment. Alec and Frank became busy with all the practice they had to do out of hours in order to achieve the required proficiency of 25 words per minute. They often stayed up very late. Thanks to sheer fatigue, there were a few times when Alec went sleepwalking. On one occasion he'd made it halfway to Hudson's timber yard before his mother caught up with him and woke him up.

Work went on. Wireless school went on. And so did the war. Even for Alec the war went on. The government had instituted compulsory military training for all boys as soon as they turned fourteen. For two nights each week Alec served in the 'Boys' Army', undergoing training at the drill hall in Glebe. Even if it hadn't been obligatory, he would probably have volunteered anyway. That's just the way things were. Once the war started, most lads wouldn't have dreamed of not being 'in it' in some form or another. And the news from the Dardanelles had strengthened Alec's resolve to volunteer.

Nonetheless he was still too young, and had to continue working. In the middle of 1915 Alec saw a better chance for himself at Woodhead's in Bathurst Street, and took a job in mechanical work. This lasted until 1916, when he got a job as an improver in motor and electrical engineering at Brown & Co. It was around this time that he learned — just through idle conversation with a mate at work — that Canberra had been made Australia's capital a few years before, albeit with very little in the way of settlement there, even now. Only now did it strike Alec how isolated he had been up in the Clarence district. He had not known such things. The only thing he had known was that he got up early, milked cows, went to school, and then got home and milked more cows. Now he was more determined than ever to go and see the world.

The war dragged on — much longer than anyone expected — and by mid-1916 Alec knew he *had* to be in it. At the outset, patriotism had very little to do with his desire to enlist. What did King and Country mean to a boy of sixteen? No. It was adventure he was after, pure and simple, and the chance at long last to have a good job with good pay. Alec knew that the only way he could get such a job was to become proficient at wireless operation. They wouldn't take a sixteen-year-old otherwise.

CHAPTER SIX
C'mon Boys!

They sat for their Wireless Certificates up at the Wireless Station at Pennant Hills. Frank was a little older than Alec and got his without a hitch, but despite the fact that Alec passed the exam with flying colours he wasn't granted the certificate. Sixteen was too young, they said. Alec was devastated. He had spent so much time and money at the Marconi School, he could not believe the injustice. To add to his sadness, Frank and he parted company immediately, when Frank got into the Royal Australian Navy. Well, Alec thought to himself, if the Navy doesn't want me, maybe the Army does.

Evidence of the Army's recruiting campaign could be seen everywhere. Out in the bush they conducted a lot of marches, run by volunteers. They'd march from one small town to the recruiting depot in a bigger town, collecting volunteers along the road. At the height of it there was a great deal of enthusiasm. In Sydney itself there were posters everywhere. Although most of the blokes who joined up did so for adventure, or because their mates had enlisted, Alec had to admit that the recruiting posters did spur their sense of patriotism along a bit, including his own. More than anything, though, was the lure of six shillings a day. Six bob a day tended to prompt boys like Alec into enlisting far more than any motive of patriotism could.

Everyone in Australia had been shocked at the tremendous casualties at Pozières, on the Somme, and a lot of posters appealed to young blokes to go and avenge them. At the same time, there was the occasional poster that would make you think twice, such as the one up the road from Alec's house in Glebe which read, 'Your King and Country Need You' — to which some wag had added, 'But the buggers never feed you'.

The Army had been advertising particularly for wireless operators to go to Mesopotamia. Where Mesopotamia actually was, Alec had no idea. Having decided to put his age up to eighteen, he trotted down to Sydney Town Hall and became just another face in a long queue. All manner of men were queued up in front of him. Old and young. Thin and fat. Townies and boys from the bush. And other boys of sixteen. Boys who had only recently begun to shave. As Alec neared the reception desk, he was gripped by panic as he laid eyes upon the recruiting officer. Of all the men it could have been, why did it have to be the area officer in charge of Alec's cadet unit? He knew exactly how old Alec was!

To have departed the queue and made a run for it required courage. To have remained in the queue and gone through with it required both courage and stupidity. Alec chose the latter. Within moments he was standing before the desk. The minutes he waited while the officer scribbled some notes on some official-looking forms seemed like hours. Finally the officer looked up, smiled instant recognition, and said, 'Hullo, Griffiths. What are you doing here?'

'Oh, I've come ... I've come ... to enlist, sir,' Alec stammered.

'Is that right?' The officer made the knee-patting gesture of a man about to leave. 'Take my advice, Griffiths, and go home and sleep for a few years.'

Unhappy but undaunted, Alec resolved to join up, whatever it took. The next day he took himself down to Marrickville Town Hall to enlist, and wrote down his age as eighteen and six-twelfths. For some reason he had no trouble in joining up immediately; indeed, he was welcomed with open arms. The recruiting staff had surely known that he was well under eighteen and a half, but the instant they learned that he was a trained wireless operator they forgot about his age. By 1916 the Services were so desperately short of wireless operators, due especially to the high casualty rate among operators in the trenches, that they were taking just about all comers. It was that easy. After a cursory medical exam at Victoria Barracks at which his weight, height, and chest and waist measurements were taken, Alec was accepted and swore to '... well and truly serve our Sovereign Lord the King in the Australian Imperial Force from 20th September until the end of the War ...', and to '... resist His Majesty's enemies and cause His Majesty's peace to be kept and maintained ...'. At last, he was 'in it'.

The Army had no problem in enlisting thousands of keen young lads like Alec Griffiths. The problem it did have was where to accommodate them all. Alec said goodbye to what remained of his family at home in Glebe and spent the first night out at the Showground, where he slept in a horse stall. There were no pavilions at the Showground in 1916. Just horse stalls. A palliasse and two horse blankets formed his bed. Although he slept on clean straw, the ground beneath was so saturated with horse urine that no amount of straw could prevent the stench seeping through and permeating his clothes. After a few days he was issued with uniforms, equipment and iron-studded boots. At last he looked like a soldier, even if he felt more like a live-in stable hand.

From the Showground he was sent to do his basic infantry training out at Liverpool. Since he had given his occupation as wireless operator, Alec spent only about a week there — doing drill, practising musketry on the range and learning about hygiene and diseases — before being sent down to the Engineers Depot at Moore Park. As there was very little he didn't know about wireless, he was immediately placed on one week's notice to go to overseas.

At Moore Park the wireless section of which Alec was part was getting ready to go to Mesopotamia or Egypt. This brought to three the number of weeks between Alec's enlistment and possibly being sent off to war. The men were instructed in the operation of the pack wireless, a set which could be mounted on the horses, camels or mules used in the desert. The wireless set itself was placed on one side of the animal, and a petrol engine on the other, so that the whole lot straddled the beast's back like two enormous panniers. To use the set, the operator had to place the equipment on the ground, and insert a drive shaft between the two main components. The whole thing felt as if it weighed a ton. And some smart alec in the Army had had the hide to call it a *portable* set! Alec reckoned the poor mules wouldn't agree.

Besides wireless training, the unit did a tremendous amount of bayonet training. Alec couldn't work out why wireless operators would ever need to use a bayonet, but that was not the sort of thing you questioned. With rifle and bayonet fixed, they had to charge, yelling as they went, towards the end of the course before shoving the bayonet into a bag of chaff. They all got it right the first time, but this didn't stop the instructing staff from making them do it over and over again. For a week at the Showground Alec had slept on chaff bags filled with straw. At Moore Park he was running towards chaff bags, screaming at them, and running them through with a bayonet. In his sleep he began to see chaff bags coming towards him. He swore to himself that he would never lay eyes on a chaff bag ever again.

* * *

After a week at Moore Park, Alec cobbered up with a bloke by the name of Bob Lauchland. Alec liked him at once. Bob was a tough, wiry little Queenslander, a good deal older than Alec. His face had been tanned by the relentless Queensland sun, and this accentuated his brightness of eye and the cheeky turn to his mouth that Alec immediately associated with the cockies back up north. He had been in telegraphy with the Post Office.

'Stick close to me,' he said, 'and you'll be right.' Bob was Alec's guide, his confidant, his friend. His best mate. Within a very short space of time they both knew they'd be *best* of mates for life. That's how it was in the Army — you went through that much together that you'd end up being mates with some of the blokes in no time at all. Bob took Alec under his wing like he was his younger brother.

They were a few weeks into their training at Moore Park when the commanding officer came over during a smoko, while they were all having a yarn. Lining up the whole squad, he didn't waste time. He just said, 'Look here, fellers, I want volunteers to go to the Australian Flying Corps.'

Aviation was still very much the new thing, and its inherent dangers were well known. The men looked at each other quizzically. Some of them smirked. Most of them guffawed.

'Volunteers?! Flying Corps? That'd be suicide.'

'Gee whiz, that's the last thing you'd wanna go to. It's too dangerous!'

'All right,' the CO said curtly. He sucked his teeth. 'If I don't get anybody, I'll just have to detail the men I want.'

As though it was choreographed, everyone averted their eyes from the CO at precisely the same moment and stared at the ground, as if by doing so they would suddenly become invisible. Everyone, that is, except for Alec and Bob. They looked not at the ground but at each other.

'If we don't volunteer they'll probably break us up,' Bob ventured.

'Yeah. They'll take one of us and not the other,' added Alec.

Being the youngest of the two, Alec was reluctant to say anything further. This was a big decision after all. But he couldn't help himself. 'So why don't we both go!' he blurted out.

Bob said nothing. He just winked at Alec, and they knew immediately that they were both in it together. Perhaps Bob had aviation in his blood. Alec didn't. Sure, he'd heard about aeroplanes. But he'd never actually seen one. Alec had no idea what an aeroplane even looked like.

He would soon find out. Out of their squad, the two of them were the only ones to volunteer for the AFC, and from the looks on their cobbers' faces, Alec figured they must have thought the two of them were short a bob or two. From the expression on the CO's face, he must have thought they were insane too.

The Australian Flying Corps moved quickly. Perhaps too quickly. Within hours Alec and Bob were being unceremoniously bundled onto a train to Laverton in Victoria, before they could get cold feet and change their minds. It was Alec's first interstate trip.

The bleak atmosphere at Laverton made them feel irritable and uneasy. What there was of the sky was a mere blue ribbon on the horizon, on the edge of a carpet of menacing black cloud. When some of the cloud dissipated, it were as though the ribbon had been tied into a deformed bow, and it wasn't long before the bow squeezed a rainstorm out of the clouds. Laverton was nothing more than an open, windswept paddock, furnished with a solitary iron shed and a number of bell tents. It struck the lads that it was not unlike pictures they had seen of an Indian wigwam village, only less hospitable. When the wind blew, the sides of the tents billowed in and out violently, reminding Alec of the parchment-faced men at Circular Quay who sucked their cheeks in and out as they wistfully watched vessels plying Sydney Harbour. The bell tents received the full force of the volatile spring weather and the lads really felt its chill as they slept with their feet to the centre-pole, eight men to a tent. They would awaken to feel their toes beautifully warm, and their heads almost frozen.

They were in the Flying Corps, but they did everything else but fly. The only aeroplanes Alec ever saw at Laverton were a Bristol Boxkite and a pusher-engined Maurice Farman Shorthorn. At least, he *thought* that's what they were. He didn't much care exactly what they were. All he knew was what he had been told: whatever they were, they were now — even by this stage of the war — 'old' planes.

For a month the men lived in their 'wigwams', spending the days doing routine drill and fatigues. Alec's fatigue duty was invariably peeling potatoes. Not just a few, but hundreds. No leave was granted, and life for the men posted to Laverton was very, very monotonous. They knew that the city of Melbourne lay not too far away to the east, yet most of them would never even get to drink in its fabled pubs. So tedious was life that they held a mock ceremony to 'officially' proclaim their AUSTRALIA shoulder badges as standing for 'Are U Satisfied To Remain At Laverton In Agony?' The only attempt made by the AFC staff towards relieving the monotony was to send the men out on route marches. 'It'll keep you happy,' they told them. Perhaps it was their idea of a joke.

Because the staff failed to relieve the boredom for the men at Laverton, a mate of Alec's decided that he would. He was the camp bugler, and instead of marching onto the parade ground and blowing Reveille each morning he would just lie in bed, slide back the tent flap, and blow. Each day for a month the men heard every conceivable 'tune', note and noise except Reveille. On some mornings his attempt might sound vaguely like Reveille, at other times like a klaxon horn being blown underwater. But no matter what it sounded like, the fits of laughter the bugler's attempts induced ensured that they all got up immediately. It was the bugler himself who was always last out of bed.

Relief came when their overseas embarkation orders arrived. Their destination was not revealed to them, and furphies spread through the camp like a bushfire. But it didn't really matter where they were going, so long as it was overseas.

Alec signed some papers that authorised two-fifths of his pay to be sent to his mother, and one shilling per day to be held over until his discharge. Second class air mechanics were paid eight shillings per day, infantrymen were paid six. The commanding officer lined the men up and told them the unit name by which they were to be known: the Second Reinforcement to the 2nd Squadron, Australian Flying Corps. (The 2nd Squadron itself had already departed for overseas on the A-38 *Ulysses* about a month earlier). Alec's unit consisted of approximately twenty tradesmen covering all manner of trades connected with aeroplanes. If truth be known, few of them were particularly concerned about what they were called. They just wanted to get off to the war before it finished. Indeed, they were almost unhappy about the week's embarkation leave they were granted before they left.

With the fragrance of the coming summer came sailing date — 23 November 1916 — and the lads, especially Alec Griffiths, were filled with a mixture of excitement and trepidation. Excitement because they were going overseas, trepidation because they were going off to war. And Alec had yet to turn seventeen.

Above all, they were filled with relief. Their time at Laverton had been less than enjoyable and they were glad to be out of there. Morale escalated as they all filed into the back of a Leyland motor lorry fitted with solid rubber tyres, and they sang 'Baby Doll' and 'Australia Will Be There' on the way down to Port Melbourne. Their thirst for adventure was at long last to be quenched.

PART II

THE GREAT WAR

CHAPTER SEVEN
Destination Unknown

At the wharf, what seemed like thousands of soldiers were queuing up to embark on the ungraceful bulk of His Majesty's Australian Transport *Hororata* (A-20), fitted for some 60 officers, 2000 soldiers and more than 120 horses. The ship's maximum speed was fourteen knots, and it was owned by the New Zealand Shipping Company Ltd. The moment Alec laid eyes upon it he recognised the ship as the one he'd been designing in his head for the past week. The *Hororata* was the offspring of the quaint coastal steamer *Kyogle* of his youth, and the archetypal South Seas freighter of his imaginings. It was anything but handsome, in fact it was as unalluring as it was untouched by recent paint. But it was solid, and curiously reassuring to a soldier. Her myriad portholes just below the gunwales were redolent of the eyelets on an Army boot.

As each pair of men approached the gangway their papers were checked by the boarding officer. It wasn't long before the men were making light of their method of boarding, two by two. 'Thank you, Noah,' one said. 'What was that?' barked the boarding officer. Smiling and ever so courteous, the soldier replied, 'I said, "Thank you ... sir".'

Alec's papers showed that he was eighteen and a half, but he was now to learn that this didn't guarantee him a trip overseas. Parental consent, it turned out, was required if you were under nineteen and wished to go abroad on active service. This he did not have. Alec pleaded with the boarding officer. He had come this far; he was not about to have his plans to go overseas and 'be in it' dashed without a fight. A frantic message was sent to Laverton to find a replacement; so scarce were wireless operators that the *Hororata* was not going anywhere until a replacement was found for young Griffiths.

For four hours the ship's departure was delayed solely on Alec's account. The pale beach of wellwishers' faces on the wharf was awash with smiles, for their loved ones were being accorded a four-hour reprieve. Finally, when it became apparent to the boarding officer that no replacement was going to turn up, he placed his hand on Alec's shoulder, handed him back his papers, and with a 'Best o' luck, son!' let him scramble up the gangway just as it was being withdrawn into the bowels of the ship.

Among that sea of smiling faces on the wharf there wasn't one face that Alec knew. He waved anyway — it seemed to be the right thing to do. Just as the ship was pulling away from the pier Alec saw his replacement arrive in a lorry. The man jumped out and gazed up at the deck. Alec waved to him. He was quite a good cobber of his from Laverton and Alec knew how desperately he wanted to go overseas. The friend did not wave back. He simply stood there, staring at Alec, arms akimbo.

The men were in high spirits as they steamed down Port Phillip Bay and out through the Rip. Seagulls alternated between relaxing on the railings and conducting their arcing searches of the sea's unknown for food. For many of the ship's crew, the unknown would begin when they arrived at their destination. For the soldiers, the unknown began now. They lined the sides of the ship, jostling for position with each other along the railing. Rough weather in Bass Strait slapped them in the face and set their peaked caps to a windswept, jaunty angle not long after the sinewy green and brown fingers of Point Lonsdale and Point Nepean had disappeared beyond the *Hororata*'s churning wake. This weather, and what was to follow in the Bight, would soon dampen these high spirits. Compared with his mates, Alec (whose experience of the sea had been confined to two coastal voyages and a handful of afternoons spent standing, trousers rolled up, in the broken surf of Sydney's beaches) was an old sea dog. For almost all of the men this was their first sea voyage, and many of them would spend a lot of it hanging over the side. The living conditions aboard the *Hororata* did not help. The crew spent most of their time simply looking up at the sky and saying not very much at all.

Being an old cargo ship, the *Hororata* possessed little in the way of accommodations. A more unloved and unlovable vessel had never sailed. There were four stinking cargo holds, each with two lower decks. The bottom decks were well below the waterline and had no portholes. They reeked. From the main deck the men went down a makeshift narrow wooden staircase to A deck, and then down another to B deck. Here there were a lot of wooden tables, each about ten feet long with a wooden 'lip' built in on each side, and fixed in position running from the side of the ship towards the centre. Each table accommodated a section of twelve men. They all had to take turns as mess orderlies, whose job it was to go up onto the open deck, collect the food for the section, and bring it back down the stairs and see that what remained of it after the pitch and roll of the ship was equally distributed. The orderlies went to the store each morning at about 1000 hours (ten o'clock) to collect the day's dry rations — bread, butter, cheese and jam.

For the midday meal they often got a plate of mutton stew and a boiled potato, but only if the weather was fine. If not, the men were given Maconochies tinned stew, consisting of lumps of fat ('meat'), carrots and sliced turnips floating in a thin gravy, and eaten cold. After a few days of cold Maconochies, it became a standing joke between Alec and Bob. 'We're condemned men, cobber,' Alec would say, grinning broadly and knowing full well what Bob's reply would be. 'Yep, I know, cob! Condemned to a watery gravy!'

The cookhouse consisted of a number of boilers on the open

deck, fired by coal. They were useless in rough weather because spray came up over the ship's gunwales, extinguishing the fires. It was ironic really, Alec realised before too long. In fine, warm weather they could have done without a hot meal, but there was always one on offer. In cold and rough weather they yearned for a hot meal but there was Buckley's chance of getting one. At least they were always assured of a nice hot cup of tea, as it was brewed in a boiler which was heated by steam from the engine-room boiler. Each table was supplied with two large dixies, and these held enough food and tea for all the men of the section.

Discipline was strict. The duty officer came around each morning to inspect everything and ensure that all was in order. It was the orderlies' duty to scrub the table white prior to inspection and arrange the utensils in their 'stormproof' racks. If all was not to the duty officer's satisfaction, the orderlies were for it. And if the orderlies were for it, so were the other ten men in the section. But usually they all looked after each other and there were seldom any problems.

Each of the men fought a constant battle to maintain hygiene. The only washbasins were up on deck, with only salt water coming out of the taps. There was no fresh water whatsoever with which to wash; even the rare shower they were permitted was with salt water. The only available fresh water was for drinking, and even then only at certain strictly enforced times of the day. It was simply bad luck if you wanted a drink of water at other times, unless you had the foresight to fill your canteen. Nor were there any latrines below decks. You had to go up top to use the 'latrine facilities', which consisted of nothing more than a long wooden platform built over the ship's gunwales, with holes at three-foot intervals. They emptied straight out over the side into the sea. Often there'd be eight or nine blokes all sitting along it at any one time, which made for some pretty interesting conversation. But it was a most unpleasant experience if anyone had to go at night, especially if it was blowing a gale.

At night they slept in canvas hammocks slung from steel hooks all the way along the bulkhead in their 'accommodation area', the cargo hold. Each man was supplied with a horse blanket and a kapok-filled life jacket for a pillow. Once the hammocks were slung there was barely a hair's breadth between them, not only in the middle but also at both ends, since the tapered ends fitted alternately into each other. As a result it was decided by Alec's section and the neighbouring sections that they would sling their hammocks in a particular order from the same numbered hooks each night. If you were unlucky enough to have a neighbour who snored, that was just tough luck. After the hook allocation, you were stuck with him for the remainder of the voyage. Nevertheless, the numbered hammock system soon proved a workable solution to a hefty problem, unless a few of the men were off in another section playing cards or two-up until late. Pandemonium would erupt on their return as they crawled under Alec's mates' hammocks in the dark trying to find their own possie. Making matters worse was the fact that they also had to negotiate an obstacle in the middle of the deck: a large steel trunk, into which the hammocks were rolled up and placed each morning.

By Albany, the first port of call, the noise of the hammock rings rubbing against their hooks had driven half the men a bit crazy. Sleep below decks was as elusive as silence. The other half were as crook as dogs from the movement of the Bight's relentless, seething seas, having spent much of the voyage parking their Maconochies (looking little different on the way out than it had on the way in) over the rail. Any respite they may have expected on anchoring in King George Sound was not to be found, for they were not permitted ashore. The *Hororata* took on fresh water and supplies, which were brought out to the ship on big barges. Despite not being granted leave, some of the boys did manage to stow away on the empty lighters and get ashore for a couple of days. One chap in Alec's section could not stop himself from boasting about what a good time he had had while ashore. He had met a girl. When he had to leave she had given him some of her old clothes to wear so that he could avoid being caught by members of the Provost Corps — the military policemen.

Other ships in King George Sound had been awaiting the arrival of the *Hororata* and now, as they all steamed westward, they shook out into a convoy of about nine vessels. The theory behind the convoy formation was that they would be afforded a certain amount of protection against submarines and raiders. Furphies were rife that enemy U-boats, and possibly some German raiders, were operating just off the Western Australian coast, and that the Australian vessels would be in the 'danger zone' all the way to their destination. Whether submarines actually got anywhere near Australia was questionable, but everyone was playing it safe.

None of the lads knew what their destination was. On weighing anchor in Albany they had been informed that they were heading for 'Destination Unknown'. This very ship had been part of the First Detachment of the Australia and New Zealand Imperial Expeditionary Forces which departed this very same Sound on 1st November 1914, and as many of the lads called to mind that those boys had gone on to the Dardanelles, they realised something: now, as the *Hororata* left Albany in the distance for 'Destination Unknown', it was to be the last time many of them would ever see the beautiful Australian coastline. Only one naval escort shepherded the frail convoy — Convoy No. 27 from Australia — the British cruiser HMS *Glasgow*, which steamed on ahead. The *Glasgow* could do about 25 knots and had 6-inch guns. At night time absolutely no lights were permitted in the convoy except a small, dull navigation light on the side of each ship. Some of the ships were faster than others, making it very awkward for the group to maintain their assigned positions. The dearth of light made the task all the more difficult, and each morning Alec would look around to see ships strewn all over the place. And where there should have been nine vessels there were frequently only five or six. Rumours as to the fate of the missing ships would spread among the men like bushfire until eventually someone spied smoke on the horizon and they would all cheer. No doubt the lads on the other transports did the same thing when they finally saw the *Hororata*, Alec thought. It was one of the slowest vessels in the convoy.

The surface-raider and U-boat threat meant that the men were under very strict orders at night. No lights were to be shown whatsoever. Even cigarettes were forbidden on deck. All the portholes were ordered closed and blacked out. As a result it became very stuffy and oppressive down below for some. For Alec's section, it made no difference. It was stuffy for them all the time, being below the waterline and having no portholes. Occasionally the officers would permit them to take their hammocks, blankets and life jackets up top and to sleep on deck. This brought welcome relief from the oppressive heat in the cargo hold, but it also brought hazards.

Every morning, very early, the crew washed the decks down with a hose. They were a foreign crew — from India, Alec reckoned — and they called all the troops Johnny, regardless of rank. The men would hear them coming just before dawn broke, singing out 'Wash deck, Johnny! Wash deck, Johnny!' When the lads heard that, they moved quick smart to get out of bed and furl their hammocks. Failure to do so within two minutes resulted in a thorough soaking. Before they got wise to this, however, Bob and Alec caught the drenching of a lifetime. They laughed about it for days.

The pair got to know each other even better during the voyage. They soon became like dinky-di brothers, inseparable. They always teamed together in games of cards. They always yarned to each other whenever they didn't have duties to perform. A lot of the other men even asked them if they were brothers. Some days out of Albany, Alec had a new experience, the like of which he could only have dreamed of back at the dairy farm at Lower Southgate. Just as the sun, tired after the effort of gilding the horizon all day, was dropping into the sea, Bob spotted some flying-fish beneath the bows. He told Alec what they were, but Alec was convinced he was pulling his leg. Alec swore that they were birds that periodically spiralled down beneath the water to catch a meal. But sure enough, closer scrutiny revealed that they were indeed flying-fish. They were soon joined by porpoises — dozens of them — playing in a sea as smooth as a sheet of glass. The war seemed far away.

Many of the boys had expected the journey to be not unlike a pleasure voyage abroad. In some respects it was, but they still had to attend church parades and full dress parades as though still in barracks, and physical training every morning on the crowded, rolling deck. These sessions were more amusing than they were physically beneficial. Duties had to be performed, day and night. One was fire guard, which meant continually walking around the *Hororata* from stem to stern and back again, looking for fires. Some of the blokes on fire guard wished to find a fire — or better still light one — just to relieve the monotony of the duty. As the *Hororata* was a coal-burning ship, the officers would often randomly select soldiers for duty in the boiler room to assist the firemen in shovelling coal into the fires. Another duty entailed standing guard outside the sick bay. Alec's first stint there occurred some weeks after Albany and he noticed that the bloke who had stowed away on a barge had become a patient as a result of his good time ashore. A set of clothes, it seemed, was not the only thing the lady had given him. When Alec spoke to him, he was not nearly so enthusiastic about the pleasures of Albany as he had been on his triumphant return to the ship.

But the main duty was submarine guard. This was a permanent picquet mounted throughout the daylight hours. Men were stationed on both sides of the ship at regular intervals along the deck. They clustered along the railings, a sense of expectancy heavy in the air. The ship must have been quite a sight from the water, had the porpoises cared to look up. Every man got a turn at this job of watching for periscopes. They were each armed with a loaded rifle and had orders to fire on any periscope that appeared. How they could be expected to sink an enemy submarine with a rifle was a source of amusement to them all, especially as none of them had any real idea what a submarine looked like.

'I see yer on tin-opener duty again, cobber,' a passer-by said to a rifleman.

'I tell ya, mate, by the time a Hun submarine gets within rifle range, the last bloody thing I'll be thinkin' of is shootin' at its periscope!'

'You're right. What the blazes is a beriscote anyway?'

The monotony of submarine guard gave way to excitement when the lads sighted land — the southern coast of Africa. As they drew closer they could make out the unmistakable shape of Table Mountain. They had heard all about this landmark from a South African crewman. It was a welcome sight to see a young girl perched right out at the end of the breakwater in Cape Town, waving a flag at the boys. (Later they learned that she was the harbourmaster's daughter and that she welcomed all troopships in the same way.)

The euphoria was short-lived when the boys learned, once again, that they were not to go ashore. While coal, stores and water were taken on, they had to content themselves with watching the activity on the wharf. Two wooden planks were laid up against the ship, one at each end. Dozens of men — 'coolies' the troops called them — each carrying a basket of coal on his head, gingerly negotiated the 'up' plank, tipped their loads into large bins, and walked along the deck and off the ship on the 'down' plank. This continued night and day until the bunker was full, but the officers nonetheless deemed it prudent not to allow shore leave.

And so the boys decided to create their own amusement, any pranks they could think of, just to relieve the boredom. While the coolies were on their lunch break they sat on the wharf and gazed up at the white faces on the ship, eagerly awaiting the scraps of food they had evidently grown accustomed to getting from other troopships. One of the lads from Alec's section decided to throw pennies down to them, and then a few others joined in. The coolies scrambled for the pennies and the boys got their amusement. It wasn't long before this idea became a bit stale, so the boys hit on the idea of putting the pennies on the stove for a while before throwing them down to the wharf. The first coolie to catch a hot penny had to throw it away immediately, clutching his hand. Another, who hadn't yet caught on, would then pick up the dropped penny, burn himself a little too, and throw it away. And so on. Some of the boys laughed so hard they fell to the deck, clutching their sides. Eventually the coolies learned to toss the hot penny from hand to hand until it cooled down, and then they were happy.

Soon the hot penny game also got stale, though some of the boys continued to throw a few coins over the side. Just as they thought their entertainment had dried up, some wag hit on another idea. 'Who's got a bunger?' he sang out. As quickly as if they were being presented for an inspection, bungers were whipped out from everywhere — pockets, kitbags and even hats.

'Strike me handsome,' the prankster exclaimed. 'I only asked fer one o' the bleedin' things!' He looked thoughtful, as if about to conduct a science experiment at school, and then smiled. 'Right-oh. I need a loaf o' bread.' Within seconds one appeared. Most of the boys hadn't seen much fresh bread during the voyage, but someone obviously had. The wag scraped out the inside of the loaf and put the bunger in. With surgeon-like skill he then stuffed some of the bread back inside the crust, leaving a small part of the bunger's wick protruding.

'Right, fellers! Cop a load o' this,' he called out, lighting the wick and hurling the loaf down to the wharf in one deft movement. One of the coolies caught the bread and, as he stood around waiting for more, laughed at his friends still juggling hot pennies. When he realised there was no more bread coming his way he tucked the loaf under his arm and walked away, looking particularly pleased with himself.

Crump! The bread exploded, and so did all the other coolies — with laughter. As seagulls swooped down onto the thousands of breadcrumbs, the prankster yelled out, 'Take it easy, y'ol' bastard!' The victim smiled. The expression on his face was worth more to the bored soldiers than all the wealth of the Indies.

CHAPTER EIGHT
Dumb Insolence

By the time Cape Town was no more than a speck in their iridescent wake the ships of the convoy had been joined by two more. They still only had one armed escort — that was all the Royal Navy could spare. Formed up line abreast, in two columns, the ships were still headed for 'Destination Unknown'. For the next couple of weeks the voyage was uneventful, save the burial at sea — to the tune of 'Nearer My God to Thee' — of the inedible Christmas dinner (pieces of fat, bones and potato floating in a stone-cold mixture of fresh water and sea water), and Alec's last sighting of the Southern Cross. The prospect of never again seeing her reassuring lights had torn at his heart.

Now, Alec became involved in an incident that would, for him, make the rest of the trip anything but uneventful.

A handful of sunsets before they called into Sierra Leone, Alec was sent to mount guard duty outside a storeroom door at the end of a long passageway. He was furnished with a rifle — bayonet fixed — and given the order to let no one inside. A notice on the door read: 'Strictly No Admission Without Permission'. After the first hour Alec was curious, not as to what the door concealed but as to why he was guarding a heavily locked door. After the second hour, curiosity abdicated and boredom reigned. There was no sound but the ceaseless vibration of the engines driving the vessel ever onward to 'Destination Unknown'.

A few more hours had passed when an infantry officer marched along the passageway towards the door, straight towards Alec. Alec didn't say a word, believing discretion to be the better part of doing what you're flamin' well told. He simply pointed at the sign. But the officer — whose Sam Browne belt somehow made him look more imposing than he really was — kept coming. When he was a few yards away, Alec raised his rifle and pointed it at the man's ribs. On the end of his rifle was about eighteen inches of cold steel. The officer managed to come to a stop just before he skewered himself with his own haughty momentum. The bayonet tip actually punctured his tunic. He glared at Alec without a word, made a smart about-turn, and strode away.

Fifteen minutes later he returned to the passageway with the sergeant of the guard, and a replacement for Alec. Alec was arrested and unceremoniously marched away to be confined to the guardroom, where he would spend a less than comfortable night pondering the wisdom of a sixteen-year-old kid shoving a bayonet into an officer's ribs.

Suddenly he realised it was New Year's Eve and that he would turn seventeen locked up alone in that guardroom cell, contained in a thimble somewhere in the middle of the ruffled grey fabric of the Atlantic.

The next morning — the first one of 1917 — Alec was taken under guard up to the disciplinary court held on the bridge and presided over by the *Hororata*'s captain. With his escort he waited outside until a voice boomed, 'Prisoner and escort, quiiiiiick ... march!' Alec was taken into the courtroom where he stood rigidly to attention (as he had been told in no uncertain terms to do) and stared at the panelled wall at the rear of the bridge, afraid to look anywhere else.

'1332 Second Class Air Mechanic Hugh Alexander Waters Griffiths, you are charged with dumb insolence! What do you have to say?' The captain glared at him.

'Sir, I was only doing my duty,' Alec replied, remembering the standard reply Bob had advised him to give if ever he got into trouble. 'My strict orders were to let no one into the store.'

The captain turned to face the sergeant of the guard. 'Is that right, Sergeant?'

'Yes sir, that's right sir.' The sergeant turned a light shade of red.

'Well then,' the captain said, annoyance replacing the menace in his voice, 'if that's so, case dismissed. This has been a complete waste of my time.' He turned to Alec again and said, 'You are free to go.'

Later that day, while Alec was having a yarn with his section mates on the fo'c'sle, the sergeant of the guard approached him and said, 'The captain wants to see you on the bridge again tomorrow, 0800. Be there!'

'What've I done this time?'

'Oh, don't you worry 'bout that, son. You'll see in the mornin' orright. You'll see.'

The following morning Alec was again marched in before the captain, who turned to Alec's escort and said, 'You! You may go.' Out of the corner of his eye, Alec watched the sergeant disappear and felt very exposed.

'I understand you know the Morse code,' the captain said, pleasantly enough.

'Yes, sir.'

'Are you familiar with the Aldis signalling lamp?'

'Yes, sir.'

'Good. Then if you are agreeable, I will try to obtain permission for you to come up onto the bridge and assist my ship's officers in navigating the ship.' Before Alec could reply the captain added, 'That will be all.'

Alec was detailed for duty on the bridge. The next day a cavalcade of grey clouds rolled in from some unknown place beyond the port bow, and the sun was soon breaking up in the sky. Alec was happy on the bridge, indoors. His task was mounting a regular watch with a ship's officer and dealing with any Morse light signalling between the *Hororata* and other vessels in the convoy. The watch rotation usually consisted of two hours on and four hours off. The ships were not permitted to use wireless at all now — as they were nearing Europe — in case the enemy learned their position. Consequently all signalling had to be done with lamps. This was a simple enough task during the daytime, since they could ascertain where the other ships were lying. At night, however, with the ships having the one small navigation light, the watch's task became quite difficult.

Apparently the captain was pleased with Alec's work, because Alec was able to arrange for his mate Bob (also a wireless operator) to serve on the bridge with him. Alec knew that Bob would have done exactly the same for him, and it made the rest of the voyage much more enjoyable. Instead of dossing down in the oppressive cargo hold they were given permission to take their hammocks, blankets and life jackets and sleep up on the chartroom floor. Occasionally they even scored some real food — tidbits from the officers' wardroom. It was not unlike being serfs crouching beneath the table of the medieval landowners they had read about in school, but the tucker was better than they'd been getting and they decided they would gladly suffer serfdom.

Bob and Alec never let their good fortune go to their head. They still went down when they were off duty to play two-up. For the first couple of days their mates gave them stick about being 'favourites', but it was just pulling their leg.

On the bridge one morning at daybreak, Alec spied a phosphorescent plume of water moving in the distance, and excitedly pointed it out. Foam and spray leaped everywhere. The officers on the bridge were most concerned. Every man on the *Hororata* was abruptly woken up and placed on alert. Most of them were sure they were about to be attacked. All they could do was watch and pray that the cruiser *Glasgow* could save them. As the disturbed water moved closer it became clear that the *Hororata* and the rest of the convoy were being rapidly approached by a lot of small boats. The question on everybody's lips was simple enough. Ours? Or theirs?

As the boats came nearer each one peeled off and headed for a particular vessel in the convoy, made one complete circle around it, and settled in front. There were ten of these little British torpedo boats, but looking at the one in front of the *Hororata* Alec was sure that all his mates were sharing the same thought: 'How will that dinky little thing protect us?' The flotilla of torpedo boats had come out, Alec learned, to escort the convoy into Plymouth because of the increased submarine threat near the famous English port. But the sudden sense of security he felt took a nosedive when he saw the message flashed to the convoy.

It read: 'Every ship for itself.'

For the rest of the day the *Hororata* stayed close to its little guard dog. As the convoy neared Plymouth the torpedo boats swept back astern to allow the ships to enter port. The old and slow *Hororata* was the second last in, followed by the *Glasgow*.

Alec and the other boys had been on board for nine weeks without once setting foot ashore. Taking the route through the Suez Canal and the Mediterranean would have made the voyage a little shorter, but the war made them go the long way around. Most of the recruiting posters in Australia, Alec reflected, had made war service seem like an overseas holiday. But the 'cruise' hadn't been that at all. And a lot of the soldiers who disembarked in Plymouth that day would soon be paying a very high price for their fare.

CHAPTER NINE
Should Auld Acquaintance Be Forgot

After a few grubby stations, bereft of people, they gathered speed. A spent cigarette flew past the window like a firefly. There were soldiers in a few of the compartments, smoking, joking or sleeping. The click of wheels on the rails was almost hypnotic and might have lulled Alec and Bob to sleep were it not for the passengers in their compartment who wanted to chat with the 'colonials'. At times it was a one-way conversation, as the boys had difficulty in understanding the thick accents of Cornwall and Devon. Was it truly English some passengers were speaking? No doubt the others also found parts of some of the boys' language beyond their grasp, if not a little too colourful. But the novelty value of the Australians' presence was palpable.

Alec went for a walk up and down the length of the carriage. With the exception of the Australian troops, it was a train full of women. They talked of working in mines and munitions factories and of menfolk who would never return to their village. Alec remembered the becalmed flotilla of fishing boats in the port at Plymouth; it now struck him that there were probably no men left there who could take them out each day. Indeed, Plymouth had seemed a town of the dead. There had not been a smile to be seen.

Now, as he looked out at the passing English countryside, he saw incredible beauty. He had only ever read about snow, and now he was seeing it for the first time. It was not unlike the thick frosts that had blanketed the paddocks at Lower Southgate, only more pleasing to the eye. The towns became more frequent, and the streets of the towns that they rattled through became narrower. Alec was only a little more than two months gone, but already he was missing the sight of wide bullnosed verandahs and even wider streets.

On disembarkation at Plymouth the two boys had been attached to the 69th Squadron, Royal Flying Corps. They were to make their way to 23rd Training Wing RFC at South Carlton in Lincolnshire, but first they were to be billeted in London for the night. They and their mates had not stopped talking since leaving Australia, so the brooding silence that Alec and Bob encountered when they got off at Victoria Station was deeply unsettling.

The sight of soldiers with limbs missing does things to a bloke. It was the boys' first real glimpse of what the war meant. The Tommies were standing — or sitting if they were unable to stand — on one of the platforms, smoking. A patina of dust dulled the colour of their caps and uniforms. They said nothing to each other. On another platform Alec observed a gathering of troops of about his age, talking excitedly among themselves. *Their* uniforms were crisp and new. They didn't seem to have noticed the wounded men, or if they had, they had chosen to ignore them.

By the time Alec and Bob arrived in South Carlton, having seen more wounded soldiers at St Pancras Station, Alec had done his best to jettison the image from his mind, but had only succeeded in muting it. It was an image impossible to forget.

Alec's and Bob's job was to instruct the young pilots in wireless technique. In February 1917 it was a bitterly cold place. A group of Australians had been transferred to Lincolnshire directly from service in the Middle East, and were kitted out in lightweight shirts and shorts. Several days passed before the British command arranged for them to be issued with winter uniforms and greatcoats (they were only colonials, after all), and a number of these blokes went down with pneumonia. A couple of them died without ever having heard an angry shot, let alone fired one.

The Aussie contingent were accommodated in Nissen-type huts, each of which was fitted with a coal-fired brazier. The brazier proved hopelessly inadequate, and often Alec awoke to find that his breath had condensed and frozen into tiny icicles. These hung from the roof supports above his bunk, which were only a couple of feet from his head. On some mornings the lads' boots were so frozen that they had to thaw them out by the brazier before they could put them on. While they were waiting for their boots to become pliant once more, their feet froze to the floor. Nonetheless, their accommodation here was a welcome respite from the dank, sweaty cargo hold of the *Hororata*, and Alec was thankful. Still, he had never been so cold.

While at South Carlton, Alec met a bloke by the name of Arthur Hemmings, an air mechanic who towered over Alec at six foot six inches tall. Arthur was a carpenter, and was therefore probably the busiest man in the place, employed in repairing crashed wood-and-fabric aeroplanes. The only events at the aerodrome more frequent than aeroplane crashes were Arthur's visits to the local pub whenever he got local leave. 'Tiny', as the men called him, slept in the bunk next to Alec's, so when he and his cobbers came back to camp a bit full Alec would take his enormous boots off, leave his uniform on, and heave him into bed. Alec was certain that Arthur never knew how he got to bed on nights such as these, nor appreciated the Herculean effort required of he and Bob to get him in there. But your cobbers were there to look out for you, and they wouldn't have dreamed of leaving him on the freezing floor.

From South Carlton, Alec and Bob were transferred to Perham Downs. A training school for machine-gunners, wireless operators and pilots, Perham Downs sounded interesting and the very name made it seem like the ideal rural retreat. After saying goodbye to their mates, Alec and Bob arrived at this miserably cold, wet and windy place to find a depot that made life at South Carlton seem like a holiday. You weren't posted to Perham Downs; you were condemned to it.

The better part of the boys' work here involved practising the pilots in transmitting wireless messages to the ground. For his first few days Alec was not a little self-conscious about being a seventeen-year-old kid teaching the pilots the Morse code. Then he realised that very few of them were much older. He asked one, 'Sir, what were you doing before you became a pilot?' 'Latin, French, Maths and Logic,' the young pilot replied. 'At school.' Evidently Alec had the right look about him anyway, because they listened to him intently. Not one questioned the fact that a second class air mechanic — and an Australian one at that — was instructing officers.

Bob soon obtained special leave to go up to Scotland and visit relatives there. On his return he told Alec all about the magnificent scenery and the unspeakable cold that was tempered only by the warm hospitality he'd received. He also spoke of his cousin Effie Melville with much praise and pride — in fact in much the same terms as he had spoken of Alec Griffiths to Effie. And he told Alec what had been said.

'Oh, I'd really like to hear from him,' she'd remarked.

'No, he wouldn't write to you. He's just a shy kid of seventeen,' Bob had countered.

'If I wrote him a note, would you give it to him?'

'Yeah ... I s'pose.'

And so it was that Alec received a letter from a distant admirer he had never met.

A week later he received another letter. Alec felt he was now obliged to reply. And if truth be told, as he read the lines of her letter — and in between them — he had become rather intrigued by this Scottish lassie. He crunched his way through the snow to one of the YMCA huts (labelled by the Aussies 'You Must Cherish Australia huts'), where you could get a cup of tea and do your correspondence. It was to be the first of many such letter-writing visits.

After a couple of months at Perham Downs there were very few of the original mob left — they had all been dispersed. At the time, though, the entire situation had seemed quite comical to Alec. There they were, receiving instruction on poison gas, dugouts and trench warfare, and they were supposed to be Flying Corps men. The 1916 Battle of the Somme was now history (it had also been the largest battle ever fought in history, and already books had been written and films made) but as a lot of gas was still being used on the Western Front it was decided that they would receive 'comprehensive training' in the use of gas masks in order to prepare them for active service. The training was aimed primarily at giving the boys confidence in the gas mask itself.

It was a particularly chilly morning when Bob and Alec joined the queue outside the gas hut, a long, narrow room filled with gas. Alec didn't want to go in, but then not too many seventeen-year-old boys would. Notwithstanding the fact that it was compulsory training, there was one incentive for going through early: it was preferable to standing outside in the perishing cold, looking like huddling penguins.

An instructor stood in the doorway and fitted a gas mask to Alec's face. The skin on his face had tightened due to the extreme cold, and this ensured a better-than-average seal with the mask. The idea was to walk right through to the other end just to test your mask, thereby giving you confidence that it actually worked. If it didn't seal properly, the wearer would soon know about it. Since the gas was weeping gas, a few of Alec's cobbers soon knew about it. Their masks hadn't sealed properly. The instructors made them go and do it again almost immediately. By the time they had gone through the gas hut twice, most of them felt a total wreck — they couldn't even remember their home address back in Australia. Even the name of their girlfriend often eluded them. Seeing these blokes in such a state made Alec feel overwhelmingly fortunate to have got it right the first time.

Simulation training was also conducted at Perham Downs. Some of it involved the use of a camera obscura whereby, through a hole in the roof of a hut, the trainees would see the image of aeroplanes flying overhead. For artillery observation ('art-obs'), training was conducted with the assistance of little tins of black gunpowder, which were detonated to simulate artillery shots for the pilots to observe. 'Great shot', someone would say. 'You've just blown up 27 German ants!'

Periodically Alec was also involved in target practice sessions in which the aeroplanes would dive on to ground targets and strafe them with machine-gun fire. This method of engaging ground troops in the open had already been used to great effect on the battlefields of France. The aeroplanes were RE8s, two-seater biplanes used primarily for observation but which had the capacity to strafe pretty effectively. Some pilots swore by them. Others called the RE8 'The Spinning Incinerator', owing to its tendency to spin and crash if there was inadequate ballast in the observer's seat.

Quite simply, the RE8 had to have ballast. For target practice a machine-gunner would go up. For wireless practice, a wireless man would go up. And if there was no spare body to jump in the observer's seat, Lieutenant Sandbags always went up: the turret would be filled with a number of sandbags of sufficient weight for ballast, and 'Lieutenant Sandbags' would be written on the manifest. He wasn't exactly an ace, but Lieutenant Sandbags would undoubtedly fly more sorties than von Richthofen, Brown and Cobby put together.

It was not uncommon for a machine-gunner and a wireless operator to swap over, just for a bit of variety. And at Perham Downs variety in the men's daily regimen was an essential part of remaining sane. If Alec wasn't busy, often he would go up when the pilot was conducting gunnery practice. During such practice runs the pilot would operate the main machine-gun, while the observer/gunner sitting behind would take care of the swivel-mounted machine-gun. Despite feeling like nothing more than a sandbag entangled in a spindly frame of wood and fabric, Alec reckoned there were worse things that could happen to a bloke. Being accommodated in a hut between the armourer's hut and the gunnery instructor's hut ensured that he got more than his fair share of being live ballast in the RE8s. It was much easier for the gunnery instructor to pop his head in next door and grab Alec than it was for him to scour the entire station for a spare body. Ironically, as a wireless operator based on the ground, he was to spend more time in the air than many of the young fighter pilots that were sent to the Western Front.

One day, sitting in the back seat, taxiing out on the drome to take off for a bout of gunnery practice, Alec noticed the armourer racing towards the aircraft waving his arms and shouting. 'Sir, sir!', Alec yelled to the pilot, grabbing a handful of his tunic and pointing towards the armourer. The plane came to a halt and the armourer approached Alec. 'There's some faulty ammunition,' he said, trying to catch his breath. 'I think I'd better go up this time around.'

'You're the boss,' Alec said. He got out and galloped off to the edge of the drome to watch the RE8 take off.

The first strafing run looked perfect. With the machine-gun rounds stirring up the dirt on the ground around the target, it was quite a sight to behold. The second run was even better, the target reduced to a million splinters. Then, as the pilot pulled out of his dive, the wings simply folded like pieces of paper and snapped off. Alec watched in horror as the machine spiralled three turns, slammed into the ground, and caught fire.

Instinctively, Alec sprinted across the drome to the wreck. It was the first time he had ever seen people killed, and nothing could have prepared him for what he saw. The 'Spinning Incinerator' had lived up to its name and had already incinerated the two men beyond recognition. Alec collapsed on the ground in shock; then a sense of relief swept over him. The incinerated corpse of the armourer had nearly been the corpse of a teenage lad from New South Wales. Mixed in with the shock and relief was the feeling that this would not be the last time he saw men die.

Not a great deal was known about G-forces, fatigue and stresses on aeroplanes in 1917. Aviation was still in its infancy; everything was found out by trial and error. The problem was that error was often fatal.

When the plane hit the ground the wooden propeller had splintered like a matchstick. Careful to avoid the flames, and ignoring the shouts of other men now running across, Alec rescued a couple of pieces of the propeller. He swore to himself that he would fashion a walking stick out of them as a lasting memorial to two men who had died before the Great War gave them a chance to show their bravery. And also to remind himself of his narrow escape from death.

At the Royal Flying Corps Wireless Training School at Farnborough (where Alec and Bob were posted in early July following a six-week posting to the 68th Squadron at Harlaxton) there were very few Australians. In this place of great long barracks and endless parade grounds, among countless British airmen and troops, the Aussies stuck out like bulls in a cow paddock. The sergeants and sergeant-majors loathed them and seemed to want to make their lives difficult. This served simply to steel the Australians, and in no time they had become noted for being a bit, well, 'non-regimental'. The general view was that they didn't have the discipline the others had. But they got away with it; apparently they got the job done. Alec didn't regard their lack of discipline as being of any great disadvantage to anybody. As far as he was concerned, 'the discipline *we* don't do won't matter.' Brass buttons gleaming like gold, general spit and polish, he and his mates felt, were for parades, not for the trenches or for war in the air.

For no other reason it seemed than the fact of where they were born, Australians would find themselves periodically 'marching the square'. This meant being drilled in full equipment until you gave the sergeant a mouthful of abuse and copped another punishment, or until you dropped from exhaustion, whichever came first. Many a morning Alec and Bob would awaken not to the strains of a bugle but to the echoes of a Tommy sergeant screaming, ''Eft, 'Ight, 'Eft, 'Ight! Pick 'em UPPP! You might break your mother's 'eart, you bloody colonials, but you won't break mine!' One thing could be said for such abuse: the sergeants were telling the truth in 99 per cent of the cases. Almost all of their 'colonial' charges had indeed been born in Australia, and all of those had been born prior to Australian federation in 1901. And it would not be long before a great many of them would indeed break their mother's heart, only it would be as a name inscribed on a telegram.

Despite all the abuse, Alec had a decent enough time at Farnborough. One of his mates, Bert Billings, was here with him. Bert, who had been one of Alec's instructors at Harlaxton, had previously served eight months at Gallipoli with the 1st Light Horse Brigade, and had also seen action at the Battle of Romani in 1916 before transferring to the Australian Flying Corps. He didn't speak too much about his time at Gallipoli, despite being probed by others to do so. Occasionally he would describe the fighting at places such as Quinn's and Pope's, but in the main restricted himself to talking about the general conditions on the Peninsula. Alec didn't particularly want to hear of the horrors of Gallipoli. He was pleased, however, to have an instructor who was also a cobber, and would listen willingly to Bert on the rare occasions that he allowed himself to talk about that vile place. Occasionally the two would go punting on a nearby canal. Alec found it more relaxing than the longboats back on the Clarence. Here it wasn't a matter of rushing about with oars having to row against the current, but rather just gently pushing the boat with a pole into the serenity of the evenings. And the evenings lasted a long time. Back at the depot the sergeants would order lights out before it was even dark enough to switch them on in the first place.

On the same day in late July that he got another warm letter from Effie Melville, Alec received notification that he was to join the British Expeditionary Force. Rumour had it that they'd been losing a lot of wireless operators in France and that Alec and several of his AFC mates were to be sent over to fill positions. Wireless operators were fast approaching a casualty rate of more than 50 per cent. There were furphies flying about that one of the Australian squadrons was to go to France, so Alec and Bob and the rest saw themselves as advance scouts. All they had to do was sign a few pieces of paper, undergo an inspection, and sling their kitbag over their shoulder. Only military-issue equipment was permitted to be taken abroad but, despite this, Alec put the pieces of propeller in his kitbag, which also contained all his worldly possessions. Even if he was caught, he reckoned, he could argue the point that the propeller was indeed military equipment.

The very same day that they received their embarkation orders for Europe, Alec and his mates settled back into the hard seats of the second class carriage. The smell of the wood panels — polished inadvertently by countless jacket sleeves and trouser legs over the years — permeated the carriage. Until a few of the boys lit up their Woodbines. The carriage soon filled with smoke, but there was no one to tell them off. Any of the officers they had seen embark on the same train were now luxuriating in the springy comforts of the first class carriage. Rumour hung thicker in the air than the cigarette smoke. 'We're garna France, fellers!' someone ventured. 'No flamin' way! Belgium fer shor!' came the reply. Bets were made. Money changed hands. Then, as the train pulled into its final station, both money and bets were forgotten.

The usual anti-submarine measures began as soon as their ship left Southampton. A lot of the Tommies became pretty jumpy at all the fuss, but the AFC blokes were old hands at this by now. The simple fact, they knew, was that if a German U-boat wanted them, it'd come and get them. No amount of bullets from Lee Enfield .303 rifles were going to stop it.

To try and describe the feelings of the boys as they embarked for the Western Front (they now *knew* that that was their destination, and might well be their destiny) would be futile — like trying to grab a wriggling trout in your bare hands. Happily, though, for Alec and his cobbers even the very real prospect of death didn't dampen their ability to muck about and pull legs. And the fresh young Tommies had a lot of leg for the Aussies to pull. The AFC lads told a few of their English brothers-in-arms that they'd encountered U-boats which were actually capable of clinging to the side of a ship and spouting boiling oil all over the men on board. The Tommies' fear was palpable and their 'tin-opener duty' became ever more vigilant — to the point where they were volunteering to do the Australians' submarine guard for them. Bob and Alec, too, got up to a few tricks at the expense of the Tommies, but nothing too serious. When they weren't being larrikins they were listeners. They listened to each other's life stories: their families, friends, fortunes, failures. And fears.

After the voyage from Melbourne aboard the *Hororata* — which a couple of the lads now jokingly referred to as the 'Horrorstarter' — the run from Southampton to Le Havre was short indeed. But it also felt like the longest voyage you could ever undertake. At times Alec imagined himself as one of the explorers he had learned about at school, feeling he knew something of what they must have felt so many years before, sailing inexorably into the complete unknown.

The boys reached Le Havre without incident, to be greeted by a town that — except for the countless men in khaki — did not appear to realise there was a war going on. The locals went about their daily business, scarcely acknowledging that the troops were there. They certainly didn't go out of their way to be friendly towards the Australians. Alec mused to himself that perhaps he would have been just as unfriendly had French troops lobbed into Sydney and turned *his* world upside down.

From Le Havre the AFC contingent were sent to the Australian General Base Depot at Rouelles, on Le Havre's outskirts. The Depot was more or less a big central clearing station, where all recently arrived Australians were marshalled and then sorted like fruit in a market stall. The fruit, however, was all the same colour, and none of the sorters really seemed to know what they were doing. The fruit was simply piled into railway cattle trucks according to whatever marks were visible, and sent off. There were Infantry here, and Artillery and Engineers and the like, but no Flying Corps. Everybody finally got sorted out except Alec and his cobbers — the bruised apples left sitting on their own. They stayed in this state of inactivity for a couple of days.

At length a burly sergeant approached them, wanting to find out why they were there. 'We're Flying Corps, Sergeant,' came the reply.

'Flying Corps? Flying Corps?' the sergeant said incredulously. Alec's cobber might as well have said they were Zulus. 'Do ya see any flamin' planes 'ere? There's no bloody Flying Corps 'ere.'

Someone had evidently forgotten to tell him — or the AFC. At any rate, an officer strode over to see what was going on. The group stood at attention. The officer dismissed the sergeant with a flick of his head, and dispatched the AFC men in different directions. Within seconds, Bob and Alec were separated. Just like that. They didn't even get a chance to say a proper goodbye. Alec was ordered off in the direction of the railway line, Bob Lauchland walked off in the other direction.

After a few steps Alec stopped and turned around to catch a glimpse of Bob, who touched the brim of his hat in a mock one-fingered salute of mateship. 'See ya, cob,' he shouted. Alec returned the salute and started to reply with a farewell of his own, but the words got caught somewhere between his heart and his mouth. He turned on his heel and continued walking towards the railway line, feeling not unlike the way he did on his first day of school when a tearful Eliza Jane Griffiths lovingly pushed him away. The inseparable had been separated. Parting with his best mate Bob was the hardest thing Alec had ever had to do.

At the siding he was given plenty of food and entrained in an open French Railways cattle truck with dozens of other blokes. There were no other Flying Corps men. Alec had been separated from all his AFC mates and, despite the fact that he was surrounded by other soldiers, felt very, very alone.

He was informed that he was being posted to the 2nd Division Wireless Battalion. He was told nothing more. The crunch of gravel beneath pacing army boots penetrated every seemingly interminable hour of the two days they stayed at the siding before heading east. Even once they were on the move there were so many delays due to congested military traffic and railway lines under repair that often they'd be put into a siding and left there. The train stopped in between stations more often than it stopped at them. Sometimes a few of the men would get off at a railway station for a cup of coffee and a smoko, and then walk further up the track and catch up with the train. One bloke lost the train completely by dawdling at one of the stops, but caught up with it again four miles — and four hours — further up the track. At one particular siding, just for something to do, the boys lit a fire in the corner of the cattle truck and boiled a billy. The urine-scented straw on the floor of the truck was soaking wet from recent rain, so they used shrapnel biscuits for fuel. These were found to be infinitely more combustible than they were palatable. Observing the burning 'Anzac wafers' were a couple of British soldiers. They couldn't believe their eyes, and told the Australian soldiers of how little food their chaps were getting.

The countryside was very different from what Alec was accustomed to. Instead of the familiar Cootamundra wattle, jacaranda, sugar cane and gum trees there were poplars and cherry trees. Alec remembered northern New South Wales as green and gold, whereas what he saw before him now was decidedly grey. Despite its being high summer there was no bite in the sun. The only people at work in the fields were women. Scarcely a man was to be seen in this pastoral land, save the khaki-clad figures riding around in railway cattle trucks. Except for the towns and villages the landscape was flat and uninteresting. Alec found the towns very beautiful. Although he was not a religious man, it touched him that the church always seemed to be the focal point.

When the train shuddered across several sets of points and rattled into St Omer, he learned for the first time what his destination was going to be. It was St Omer. He was ordered off the train and a Royal Flying Corps sergeant told him to make his way to the Depot. Alec had no idea where the Depot was, nor why he was being separated from the other blokes. After all, he'd been attached to the 2nd Division and not the Royal Flying Corps. He made to question the sergeant, but two icy blue eyes, deep-set into a scowling face, made him swallow his words. He slung his kitbag over his shoulder, and walked past the YMCA hut into town.

Despite the weak sunshine St Omer looked as though it had never seen a day without rain. Even the outside of the buildings looked, and smelt, damp. And many of them had been bombed. Eventually Alec was directed by an RFC wallah to the Royal Flying Corps No. 1 Aircraft Depot. The Depot was the chief source of supply for everything to do with aeroplanes that was wanted throughout the Western Front. It was a sort of a 'spare parts' depot, and supplied the needs of the different squadrons not only with mechanical replacements but with human replacements as well.

At St Omer, Alec got his first taste of war. It wasn't a taste he warmed to. He had been informed about the night bombing raids made by the Germans, but no amount of information could have prepared him for it. The method used was known as pattern bombing. How could such a devastating method of bombing come to be known by such an innocuous, almost sweet-sounding name? The 'pattern' was to be found in the formation of the aeroplanes which, flying three or four in a line, dropped bombs over a wide area. The theory was that they couldn't miss their targets. The method would in later years become the equally innocent-sounding 'carpet bombing'.

The effect of pattern bombing was invariably more ruinous than the name implied. Although there were no lights showing at night, the Germans knew either from previous missions or through their extensive spy network that there was an aerodrome or depot somewhere in the vicinity, and so would drop as many bombs as possible in order to find it. The bombs themselves were quite small; the supply of them was not. The Germans seemed to have a heck of a lot of them. Night bombing raids on the depot had been so frequent of late that each man had been assigned a particular place to go to in the event of an air raid. Usually it was a hole in the ground, or perhaps a disused cellar.

Alec's first experience of air raids occurred one night when a bomb exploded about a hundred yards away from him. It wasn't exactly a baptism of fire in the infantryman's understanding of the term, but it was Alec's baptism of fire nonetheless. He ran like blazes to his allotted trench, dived in head-first, and waited. Blood from a graze on his forehead seeped into his tunic. He could feel it but couldn't see it. Nor did he care. He was too busy being scared to care.

There are those who imagine themselves heroically facing fire for the first time. They are usually people who will never have to. Alec had never envisioned this moment in any heroic sense; he had never thought he would do anything other than what he was doing now: biting the dirt. As it turned out, he needn't have run so hard. He looked around and realised there was time aplenty to run to shelter because the lumbering German bombers were so slow. From that night on his air-raid drill became a little more leisurely. All he had to do was to make sure that he was well clear of any buildings and try to get down into a trench as soon as possible; even a ditch would suffice. That way the blast would go right over the top of him.

Although Alec was officially posted to the No. 1 Aircraft Depot at St Omer from 9 August to 21 September, it was only a few days before he commenced what was to be his job for the next six months: wireless operator in the mud, filth and misery of the Western Front. Only on paper was he truly in the Australian Flying Corps. The majority of his time would be spent with countless 18-pounder artillery batteries — and occasionally the trench mortars in the infantry trenches, the 6-inch howitzer batteries and the 9.2-inch siege artillery batteries — of the various Allied countries, up and down the whole length of the line.

CHAPTER TEN
Flanders

A silvery mist enshrouded the Flanders countryside. Alec swapped his slouch hat for his helmet, packed up his personal gear and his equipment and jumped into the motorcycle sidecar. In his kitbag were his groundsheet, knife, fork and spoon, 'housewife', toothbrush, soap, razor and lather brush, water bottle and mess tins, and shell dressing. Accompanying these — in addition to the now scrunched-up slouch hat — were a few useless items such as a comb, a spare shirt and his paybook. These could very well have been left at St Omer. Last but not least there was the locket and photograph of his mother, and his pieces of propeller.

Although it was summer he wore his greatcoat; and according to regulations he carried a gas respirator in its canvas bag on his chest. It would be his constant companion for as long as he remained on the Western Front. His equipment comprised a number of canvas strips and a Sterling crystal receiver. The latter consisted of a variable coil, a crystal detector, a pair of headphones, a twelve-foot collapsible pole and an aerial. Owing to the bulk and weight of his equipment, he was not issued with a rifle. By the time the wireless operators were carrying the wireless and their equipment, there was no way they could carry a rifle as well. But they still had to carry their canvas kitbag. Alec was happy, in a way, that he didn't have to carry a rifle. Or happy, at least, to feel sure that the time wouldn't come when he'd have to use it.

He didn't take much notice of the route he and his escort took on the journey out to the line. Such detail is of no consequence to the simple soldier. He did, however, notice that they rode along to Hazebrouck through villages bereft of both greenery and young men. To an outsider it was as though males had been banished by some local edict. A few women gave Alec and his escort a half-hearted wave as the pair passed through. In some villages, what he saw was the very picture of rural bliss. The war might well not have existed. Stone chimneys vied with the poplars for superiority over the roofs of farmhouses, pigs squealed in their sties, and the pleasant aroma of wood smoke teased the nostrils.

In other villages, one had difficulty in ascertaining exactly where individual houses and shops had stood, such was the extent of the damage. What was it that had decided which buildings would stand, and which would fall? It was the shell, the indiscriminate, impersonal, ruthless artillery shell. It cared not whence it had come and cared even less for where it was going. Yet, for such thoughtless objects, artillery shells seemed to have a mind of their own. In the fields beyond the villages carts lay up-ended, surrounded by the water of the downpours of the first week of August 1917, like shipwrecks run aground on reefs.

They flitted through Poperinghe, a sort of staging point for movement up to the line. The platform at the railway station had been smashed by heavy shellfire. Here Alec saw all manner of people — men from every corps — all waiting to move up. He watched them with a mixture of admiration and curiosity. For some, like Alec, it was to be their first time at the Front. For some it was to be their last. The men watched the motorcyclist and the sidecar's occupant intently, as if Alec was the only soldier going up to the line. What were they thinking, these boys at 'Pop', as they followed his progress?

In the ramparted town of Ypres Alec saw medieval buildings

that must once have been magnificent to behold. As he passed one in particular, the Cloth Hall, a tear welled in his eye. The once proud building stood almost alone, its spine shattered and its heart broken. Alec had heard about it from the RFC men at St Omer; they'd said it was a fine example of the 'reverse construction process', and had been getting smaller and smaller ever since the war began. Much of the rest of Ypres, quite deserted now, was not much better off.

The entire scene seemed unreal to Alec, until he heard one of the 'heavies' go off. Then another. And another. It was his first time. His escort jokingly called him a heavies virgin, and laughed. By this time Alec was crouched as low as he could go in the sidecar. The sound of just one of the big guns firing sent a shock wave right down into your core. All around him he could see the results of the Germans' heavies — huge craters in the fields and occasionally one where the road used to be. It was possible to dodge the smaller shell holes easily enough, but the bigger ones were an obstacle in themselves to be detoured around.

Finally they rode through what may once have been a crossroads, particularly pockmarked by shell holes, and headed out into the beyond. Brick dust lay heavy in the air. The fumes of high explosive bid welcome to Flanders. Accompanied by the sporadic sound of shells exploding, they continued on for quite some way until Alec heard a muffled 'There 'tis' from the rider as he gestured towards a piece of ground that looked like any other out here: cratered, rubble-strewn, muddy and devoid of vegetation.

'There's what?' Alec shouted back.

'Yer battery, that's what.'

All Alec could see were columns of shell smoke in the air, and the ruins of an old house. Quite some distance from the ruins the motorcycle drew to a halt. How it had made it this far along the muddy, shelled track was a mystery to young Alec. In Flanders all the land was very low-lying. Pitiless rain had destroyed any drainage system that had existed and almost the entire area had become a swamp. What at some stage must surely have been verdant pasture punctuated by forest was now slimy mud punctuated by black, dismembered stumps and pitted with shell holes. Yes, this was Europe, but it was not the beautiful Europe Alec had been taught about at school. The landscape he surveyed was a land as impossible to glamorise as it was hard to traverse.

'Right-oh, yer on yer own from 'ere. The BC'll brief ya when ya get in,' the rider informed him. Alec gathered his gear and dismounted. The motorcycle shot off in the direction from which they'd come. As he stood there, feeling more alone than ever before in his short life, Alec realised that he had never even learned the rider's name. He hobbled through the syrupy mud over to the battery position where a number of gunners were cleaning their 18-pounder guns. The guns were sufficiently buried to look as if half of each huge wheel had been sliced off. Some of the gunners looked as though they'd been buried at some point or other, too. One of them grinned weakly at Alec and directed him to the command post.

The battery's command post was in a dugout which, once upon a time, may have been the cellar of a house. Suspended on a rusty strand of barbed wire, a solitary brass shell case hung at the dugout's entrance and swung slightly in the breeze. Besides that, nothing moved. Alec relieved himself of his burden a few yards from the entrance, entered the dugout and carefully negotiated the 'floor' — not less than eight inches of mud. He had no idea where he was going but the daylight gradually thinned out and he could see a dim light coming from around a corner.

'Who the flamin' 'ell are you?' The voice had no face, only teeth.

'Se-Second Class Air Mechanic Alexander Griffiths, Australian Flying Corps. I'm your wireless operator,' Alec said. 'Sir,' he added.

'The BC is busy planning the next shoot. Come to the entrance and I'll brief you.' The voice was closer. 'And don' call me Sir. I work for my pay.'

Following the voice Alec headed back through the slush towards the daylight. The voice belonged to a sergeant. It no longer had teeth, just hardened gums. His weathered features and the look in his eyes made him look about forty years old, but something Alec couldn't put his finger on suggested he was probably only a few years older than himself.

The sergeant didn't tell him much. He said that the battery was shortly to conduct a shoot with the aim of hitting a crossroads just behind the German line. He added that the battery had been in this area for quite some time — he had no idea precisely how long, he'd lost track of time. The British infantrymen were relieved every few weeks and given leave behind the line. The artillery, Alec learned, seldom got much leave since they were needed not only to support the infantry but to continually conduct shoots in order to ensure that the Germans had no respite. 'Do what ya 'ave to do to set up yer equipment,' the sergeant said. 'Then wait fer further instructions.' He left Alec in the slush and returned to the relative comfort of the dugout.

At the Depot in St Omer, Alec had been advised of the time at which he was to establish wireless contact with the observer plane assigned to this sector. The idea behind art-obs was that an RE8 would fly over the intended target and transmit a code to the wireless operator. This code referred to some particular point on the ground. The method for target indication was known as the clock-ray method; the battery commander had a clock face superimposed on his map, with twelve o'clock at north. Up in the aeroplane, the pilot had to visualise an imaginary clock face on the target. Following each adjusting shell fired by the battery the pilot would send the fall-of-shot's approximate location accordingly. The 'observer' in the plane didn't take part in this. Rather he watched out for enemy aircraft that might pose a threat to the operation. Earlier in the war, observers didn't have recourse to a machine-gun, but the increased threat of aerial combat had required them to become machine-gunners, whose sole purpose was to make sure that their plane returned to its aerodrome in one piece. Thus the pilot had to do the clock-ray work and fly the plane at the same time.

Often above the crash of exploding shells, the wireless operator shouted the target indications to the battery commander who would then order corrections to the adjusting gun's fall-of-shot until an on-target round was achieved. Since the pilot had only a transmitter and the wireless operator a receiver, the only means by which the wireless operator could inform the pilot that he was receiving his messages was by laying out strips of canvas to form letters on the ground. Each letter had a different meaning.

It was to be an hour or so before Alec had to make wireless contact with the RE8. In the meantime he took in his surroundings. The battery of quick firing 18-pounders wasn't at all far back from the front line (the range of the guns being about four miles) and the effects of the battles could be seen everywhere. This sector of the line had taken a particularly heavy punishing in the previous few weeks. The whole place had been shelled almost into oblivion. Where copses of trees had once grown, now there stood only posts sticking out of the ground. Few were more than a couple of feet high. It could have been an old forest of dead stumps up near Grafton but for the fact that the country around Grafton was green. Here, in this sea of putrid mud, not one blade of grass grew and no bird sang.

The flotsam and jetsam of war lay strewn before him and behind him. Stranded wagons, their backs broken. The decaying corpses of ammunition teams' horses that had raced all the way from behind the line to make their delivery of precious yet deadly cargo but hadn't made it back. The tail of a downed aeroplane. The ubiquitous strands of wire. And dead men.

There were not more than a score of the latter, but even these few made Alec feel sick. He had been taught how to be a soldier — how to march, how to shoot. But nobody had told him how to cope with the sight and stench of dead men. They could have been Aussies. They could have been Tommies. Or they could have been Germans. Alec couldn't tell, and he couldn't really care. Out here in this wasteland the dead knew no nationality. What really struck him was that they could have been 25-year-old teachers, 40-year-old miners or 32-year-old shipping clerks. Or 17-year-old lads brought up on a farm. And they had mothers, fathers, daughters, sons, girlfriends and wives, sisters and brothers.

As he stood there, Alec wondered what his own brothers might be up to now. Were they even still alive? He could see Fred's face, jubilant at having successfully negotiated the waters of the Clarence River and kept their box of matches dry. And he could see Lock, grinning wildly, emerging from the same having swum so far underwater. They'd do it again together, one day. They had to.

* * *

The shelling, both in the distance and sometimes quite close, continued sporadically. He had a little time up his muddied sleeve before the observation machine was due to come over, and so he removed the remnants of the RE8's splintered propeller from his kitbag, pulled his jackknife from his pocket, and started to carve.

The issue knife wasn't a very good knife. At least it was strong enough to open a tin, and thus Alec felt sure that it would have to be strong enough to carve a walking stick. Rather than opening their ration tins around the edges, the Australians cut them straight across the top, and the knife did an adequate job of this. It also had grooves along the side and a hoof-pick, but Alec could not fathom why the Australian Flying Corps would be issued with a hoof-pick. It didn't take him long to learn that it was next to useless for picking mud out of the soles of his boots.

Once he'd cleaned them, it took only two steps for them to be caked in ooze again. In a way, it was no different with the vermin. Once you'd removed all the chats from your body, they'd be back again two minutes later. Alec had only been up in the line for a very short while and already the vermin had succeeded in grabbing a foothold underneath his shirt.

* * *

Suddenly, there it was — the distinctive drone of an RE8's engine approaching from behind.

Besides his transmitter, consisting of a spark coil connected to a six-volt accumulator through a Morse key, the pilot had an aerial made of copper wire, with a lead weight fastened at one end. The other end was connected to the brass centre of a reel around which the aerial was wound, which in turn was attached to the fuselage.

The brass centre of the reel was also connected to the spark coil. When the aeroplane approached Alec's battery the pilot would release the brake, allowing the lead weight to pull the aerial out to its full length — about a hundred feet. For Alec to get the best reception on his receiver, a particular point on the crystal had to be selected, within a cat's whisker. It was a very delicate trick. After a while Alec established communications with the pilot, and both got ready for the shoot.

Moments passed. The first gun fired, making Alec flinch and causing the contact on the crystal to become dislodged. He had to work fast to get it ready for the pilot's transmission. Alec received the message, indicating where the shot had landed and what correction was to be applied, and raced out into the open to lay out his canvas strips on the ground to form a letter. The pilot flew back over the battery to read the letter and ensure that his message had been received correctly. This was of paramount importance: misunderstanding of a pilot's transmission could result in the engagement of friendly troops by the artillery.

The RE8 seemed to slow as it performed a half figure-of-eight and headed back towards the target. Art-obs was particularly dangerous for the pilot and his observer because they had to keep flying back over the target and as the Germans knew they'd be coming back there was no element of surprise. Alec looked up. He admired the courage of those men held aloft above the German line in their flimsy craft, and even though he didn't like being where he was, he knew he would rather be on the ground than up in the sky with them.

After a few more rounds, heavy enemy shells began to land nearby. The battery fired again and immediately they were surrounded by bursting shells, both light and heavy. Great sticky clods of Flanders rained down on Alec constantly. Some hit him in the back, and he remembered the night of the watermelons in Grafton. Steel balls and fragments of jagged iron whirred through the air. The receiver required continual readjustment as it was constantly being jolted by the concussion from the battery's own

Australian Flying Corps personnel in England prior to embarkation for France in 1917

Alec just before he left for the war. He had this portrait taken for his mother.

Troopship *Hororata*, the ship that took Alec Griffiths to 'Destination Unknown' and the Great War (Australian War Memorial H02015)

Alec (right) and his brothers Fred (standing) and Lock

Australians soldiers pass by the ruins of the Ypres Cloth Hall on the way to the front line. Alec often passed this way to and from his various appointments with artillery batteries.
(AWM E04612)

The swamps of Zonnebeke on the day of the First Battle of Passchendaele. Alec Griffiths frequently endured similar – or worse – conditions for much of his time on the Western Front. (AWM E01200)

A view of duckboarded paths behind Australian lines, Polygon Wood. Alec Griffiths served in this area in September 1917. (AWM P0308/12/09)

A flight of Australian aircraft at the Bailleul Airfield, France. Both Alec and his brother Lock were attached to this aerodrome late in 1917 but were destined not to meet until both had returned to Australia. (AWM E01358)

An RE8 aircraft of the 69th Australian Squadron RFC (No. 3 Australian Squadron AFC), starting out for a night bombing operation. On several occasions Alec found himself flying in such aircraft during the day, facing backwards in the observer's seat. (AWM E01178)

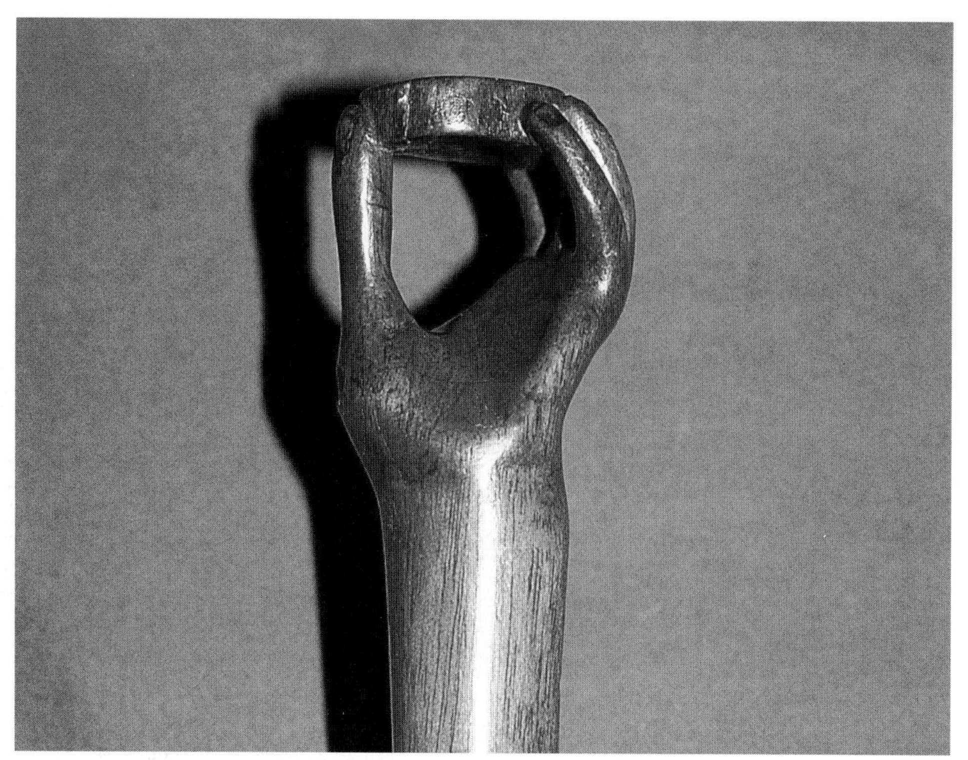

Alec's walking stick carved from the propeller blade of a crashed RE8 aeroplane (photo Rick Pfeiffer)

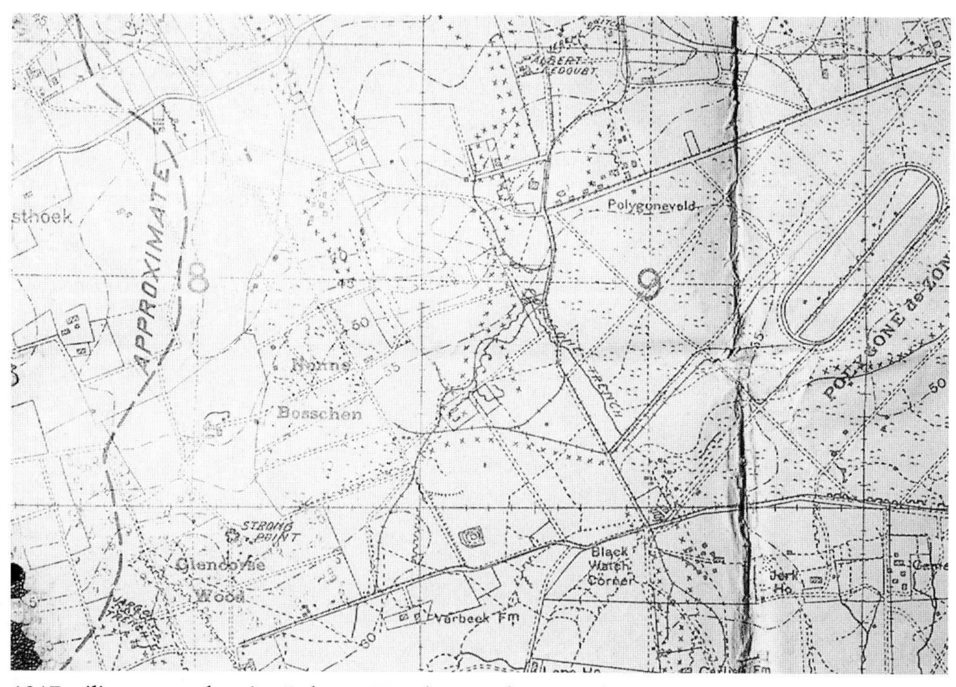

1917 military map showing Polygon Wood, East of Ypres. These maps were used by AFC pilots and artillery batteries to coordinate artillery fire. (Reproduced courtesy of 16th Field Battery RAA; photo Rick Pfeiffer)

guns and the enemy's counter-bombardment. The problem with conducting a shoot was that the battery's position was revealed to the enemy. As soon as a German plane saw either the muzzle flashes from the battery's guns or the white strips on the ground, every German battery in the vicinity would be firing at them. It was relatively safe in the dugout, and the gunners had little slit trenches to jump into when they weren't serving their guns. But Alec, after each transmission by the RE8, had to go out into the open regardless of how many shells were falling around him to lay out the canvas strips. He was the only living thing above ground when the German shells came in. But it was his job. And when he was doing it, he didn't have time to think about being afraid.

Each of the corrective sequences in art-obs generally occupied a period of five to eight minutes, and in most instances a series of up to ten such corrections were necessary to pinpoint the target accurately before the battery could fire accurate salvoes. This shoot was such an instance. Consequently Alec was out of the dugout and exposed to enemy shellfire for a total of an hour. This situation, he would learn, was to become the norm for him.

Many attempts have been made to describe what it is like to be shelled. Only those who have found themselves right in the middle of it know that it cannot really be described. Each time you hear one coming in — *hissing* in — you find yourself asking, 'Where will it land?' But a lot of the time Alec couldn't even hear them coming in until the very last seconds. Unlike an air raid, there is no pattern to it. And unlike an air raid the bombs are *big*. The scream of metal through the air is nothing less than terrifying. You don't so much hear the sound of the explosion; you feel it. You feel it in your eyes, in your jaws, and inside your head. You feel as though not only the air in your lungs but your lungs themselves are going to be sucked out. You wonder if you will ever hear again. And after the smoke and fumes have cleared and you look at the shell-churned earth around you, you wonder if you can allow yourself to be subjected to it ever again.

And yet you do. Especially to the heavies. The Germans seldom employed their heavy artillery against the infantry trenches in the front line because of the probability of a near miss hitting their own troops (so close were the opposing sides' trenches to each other) and for fear of their own trench systems being weakened. Consequently in the batteries, blokes like Alec and the gunners copped the heavies quite often. This required that the artillery dugouts be quite deep. Unfortunately they were never deep enough.

Alec was overjoyed when finally he received the message 'OK' from the RE8, which meant that the rounds were on target. He informed the battery commander, barely able to conceal his happiness. More German shells could be heard coming in and Alec waited for them to thud into the surrounding ground before racing out into the open again and laying out the letter 'T'. From that day on, T became Alec's favourite letter of the alphabet. It told the pilot, 'GO HOME.'

For the moment, however, there was no prospect of Alec's being taken away from the morass. The pilot had first to return to his squadron, inform his superiors that he had successfully completed the art-obs mission, and arrange for somebody to come out and pick Alec up. Alec waited in the dugout for the sweet sound of a motorcycle engine, all the while thinking he had been forgotten. Feeling very alone, he sat on a box and began carving his propeller pieces. For hours his world consisted of the pieces of wood, a knife, and incoming shells. He'd been told the conditions in some of the batteries were so horrific that the gunners were often relieved every day or two. As he listened to the shells exploding around him outside, he was beginning to understand why.

The motorcycle finally came when the shelling had turned from constant to sporadic. The rider had got bogged many times on the way. Instead of returning to St Omer, Alec was taken to another battery. The drizzle that had been falling all day had become rain. The rider placed his machine in the driest shell hole he could find and accompanied Alec to the dugout; he would not be riding back to his squadron in the dark and would stay the night out here, a rare event.

Two candles flickered, trying to illuminate the cramped little dugout, which had perhaps once been a farmhouse cellar. The occupants stared at Alec as though he was from another planet. He suddenly realised why: he was comparatively clean, apart from mud up to his knees and some splashes on his back. The instant he looked at the men, he knew that no one had the right to use the expression 'hollow gaze' unless they had looked into the eyes of artillerymen such as these. They looked as though even the most basic thought came only with difficulty, let alone speech. With the exception of a few mumblings between the battery commander, a 'one pip' and a sergeant, the dugout was silent. Even the sound of shelling, save the occasional shell landing nearby, could no longer be heard. If ever there was an opportunity for a man to find out if a candle's flame made a noise, this was it.

A few moments passed. Alec had a warm tin shoved into his hand and was shown where he could sit down and eat. With his jackknife he tore the tin open. He had not eaten since leaving St Omer; now he was incredibly hungry. The contents were gone in moments. Even a shell landing close to the dugout could not distract him. When he'd finished, someone pointed out an old wire mattress in a corner, indicating that he could sleep there. The mattress lay on the water-covered ground and was stained red. Alec realised that the red was the residue of blood from men fed on by lice as they slept, and the blood-gorged lice themselves. And now he discovered that the vermin were on him, too.

No special detergents existed on the Western Front to rid the men of this menace. They were always there, always on you. The lice were the only living thing in the war that Alec already hated. Even after less than 24 hours. At least there were no rats in the dugout. Sure, there were plenty around, but none in the dugout. There wasn't enough room for them. The thought of sleeping on this lousy mattress didn't appeal at all to Alec, but it was that or sleep on the floor and risk drowning in his sleep. Besides, he was already lousy right through. He laid out his groundsheet on top of the springs, and tried his best to sleep. He scratched himself every five minutes for the entire night. Even the occasional drop of kerosene applied to them didn't seem to keep them away for long. The vermin were so thick in some places that Alec swore they must have been feeding off each other.

* * *

The pre-morning was heralded by a heavy shell landing so close that Alec was sure the earth was about to open up and swallow them all. It arrived even before they had the chance to don their gas masks and 'stand to'. Shells constantly fell on the batteries, and it is true that one grew used to it after a time. To a certain extent, anyhow. But a 'heavy' was something else entirely. The heavies were so devastating that one would swear one of these shells would destroy the entire battery. By the sounds coming from upstairs, Alec gathered that there were some injuries among one of the gun detachments. He rolled out of 'bed' and his feet landed straight into about half a foot of water. Taking off one's boots at night was simply not the done thing. He was thankful for this. A bombardier soon told him that there was nothing to be concerned about and to go back to sleep.

As dawn came there was another enormous explosion nearby. Within minutes six gunners, covered in dust and mud, were brought down into the dugout, bloody fists clenched over their ears. They were screaming. Not just yelling, like a bloke who has stubbed his toe. They were screaming, *screaming*. Alec suspected that their eardrums had been shattered. Days' worth of rum ration were poured down their throats out of jars marked SRD (this stood for Service Rum Dilute, but plenty of wags reckoned it stood for Seldom Reaches Destination). The men grew quiet with shock and most lapsed into unconsciousness. Still more wounded gunners were brought down and given rum; so much so that after a while all Alec could smell in the dank air was a mixture of blood, sweat and rum. A few of the wounded who remained awake developed a sort of distant smile — almost as if they were happy to have been wounded, as their prospect of escaping the squalor they'd endured for months had suddenly increased a hundredfold.

For every five or six shells that landed, usually one was shrapnel and the remainder high explosive or gas. This one was high explosive. The shrapnel shells were the ones you really had to look out for if you were out in the open. They were capable of slicing a man in half and sometimes did.

The ensuing torrent of shells now died down to an intermittent stream. Alec shaved and did his best to clean his boots. Both tasks were an exercise in futility. He looked around for the motorcycle rider, but the man had disappeared. Alec packed up his groundsheet and was given some rations. The pommy food was woeful. Absolutely woeful. Alec reckoned the Tommies had a terrible time of things. If you wanted to eat the biscuits, you had to decide a day or two beforehand. You first had to crush them up with a rock or with the heel of your boot and then soak them in water. Failure to do so resulted in broken teeth. Fortunately Alec was also handed a tin of cold Maconochies stew, which although utterly unpalatable at least left his teeth intact.

After his meal he was briefed by the battery commander and informed that he was there to assist in conducting a shoot. This much Alec had already guessed. He was ordered to set up his equipment outside and then return to the dugout. He'd just sat down on his soaking wet kitbag when he was ordered outside again. He managed to establish contact with the aeroplane, but the signals were very weak. There was a lot of interference because all sorts of wireless sets were being used up and down the line — by Fritz as well. In a crystal set there were no valves or anything as elaborate as that, just a finicky task of adjustment. Within moments of establishing contact, the RE8 flew almost directly overhead. It headed towards some target or other in the distance. A few minutes later, Alec received the pilot's first signal and passed it on to the battery commander.

Alec had positioned his wireless set and aerial mast too close to the adjusting gun. CRACK! The gun fired, blasting the point off the crystal and rocking Alec as well. Despite its being a significant part of his job, he had received no prior training in working with live artillery, and it would be weeks before he grew accustomed to being so close to the guns when they fired.

The shoot continued. Alec grew tired racing around laying out white strips of canvas on the spongy mud. As he was doing this he wondered why the battery even bothered with camouflage. In the near distance a red enemy plane flew towards them, performed a figure-of-eight, and then flew back to where it had come from. Alec's canvas strips were easily the most visible things in the entire sector and before long the Germans were doing the same thing to Alec's battery as it was doing to them.

First, a shell landed a fair way off. Then the red plane returned. Another shell landed quite a bit closer. This continued until they were at the receiving end of a salvo. The whine of approaching shells teased Alec's ears, before the sound of explosions filled them.

No matter how many shells were falling around him, Alec kept having to leave the relative protection of the sandbags near the adjusting gun and lay out the strips to form different letters. Shrapnel from one of the German shells tore through his mast, taking a good two feet off with it. It would have to be repaired. Maintaining communications at any cost was his job.

He successfully repaired the mast and returned to the dugout to advise the battery commander. After only one more shot they were able to fire their first salvo. Alec raced out of the dugout into the open and collected his canvas strips. After that, his job was easy. The battery fired a few more salvos, the incoming shells thinned out, and then stopped. He went outside again and laid out his favourite letter — T. It had been, all told, a relatively straightforward shoot. Alec returned the observer's wave as the RE8 pilot flew back over the battery for the last time on his way to a glass of beer at whatever squadron he called home.

At the dugout the battery commander said, 'You can pack up your equipment, lad. That's it for you for today.' He added, 'Oh, and get that arm cleaned up before you disappear.'

Alec looked down at his right arm. It was covered in mud. How the blazes could he be expected to stay clean in this shell-churned morass? The battery commander continued to look at him. Alec then glanced at his left arm, to find a blood-covered sleeve. There was enough blood to make him realise that he had been sliced by a piece of shrapnel. Only now did he start to feel the combination of sting and dull ache. One of the artillerymen came to his aid, and helped him clean and dress the wound.

It wasn't a severe wound, but it was enough to hammer home to him how real all this was. His thoughts wandered to his dear mother Eliza Jane, and to his brothers and sisters. He even thought of Effie Melville, even though he had never met her. Perhaps he never would. Most of all, his thoughts turned to Bob. Alec wondered what they were all doing. He wondered if they were wondering about him.

Alec waited another night and a morning before he was picked up. Quite a lot of carving of his pieces of propeller wood got done in those long hours. He also became so lousy that he all but gave up 'reading his shirt', trying to get rid of them. One of the gunners had advised him to crush the vermin's eggs between his fingernails, but he soon gave up on this. Besides, once the lice got under your leggings they were well nigh impossible to get at. Carving was more productive. Eventually a Crossley tender arrived to take him off. It didn't seem a good idea for there to be a motor lorry so close to the line, but Alec wasn't about to question anyone's lack of wisdom. He was happy for the ride.

The driver seemed jumpy, and evidently couldn't wait to get away from the line. They drove as quickly as the shell holes in the track would allow, back towards Ypres. The muddy route had been churned up by mules and the wheels of the gun limbers. Every so often a shell or two would land close by. Alec still flinched but he now realised there was nothing to be gained by worrying about them. On the way he asked the driver about Bob Lauchland. 'Carried 'im up to that battery you've just been to, as it 'appens,' the man replied. 'Not long ago at all.' So Alec and Bob had only just missed each other.

Alec and his driver encountered columns of troops along the

way, some heading back towards the rest areas of Dickebusch and Poperinghe, and others heading up to the line. The difference in manner and appearance between the two was immense. The infantry going back for a rest from the trenches were soaked through and filthy. Alec could smell them. They had about them a look of fatalism, not unlike the look of miners' wives as they watch their menfolk disappear into the bowels of the earth. Some did their best to march. Some hobbled. Some, although hobbling, helped their mates who could neither march nor hobble. It broke Alec's heart to see them.

The driver admitted to his charge that ostensibly it was the long way round to go via Hazebrouck whenever travelling the 25-odd miles between Poperinghe or Dickebusch and St Omer (and vice-versa), but that the drivers and riders worth their salt knew this to be the better route. He didn't elaborate further, and Alec didn't ask him to. As the tender drove through Hazebrouck, heading for St Omer, Alec noticed that some of the buildings that had been there on his way out were now just piles of rubble where the German heavies had scored direct hits. On other buildings — those still standing — fine, wrought-iron grilles had become even more wrought. Once upon a time they had protected the windows from intruders. Now they couldn't protect themselves from flying shrapnel. Previously whitewashed buildings were now the colour of just-licked honeycomb. A couple of soldiers in Hazebrouck reckoned that Hun 14-inch guns had run riot. And the whole area was even more waterlogged than it had been before.

CHAPTER ELEVEN
A Country of Craters

We tenders often visit Saint Omer
To pluck young flying fishes from the 'Pool'
When in our mess there stands a vacant chair,
Late occupied by boys scarce out of school.
Our saddest days are when we cannot save,
But simply play the unofficial hearse,
As young men stand around another grave
And Padre reads the too familiar verse.

Derek White, 'The Crossley Tender'

In St Omer there was no Flanders mist. The sky had become a cloudless pale blue spectacle to be marvelled at. When Alec arrived back at the Depot, he was more or less shunned because they knew very well that he was lousy all over. He was ordered to strip off everything and go into a long hut filled with steam. He wasn't even allowed to take any of his issued kit through with him, except for his kitbag and personals. He looked down and saw red bite marks all over his body, from chest to toe. Meanwhile his old uniform was taken away and burned. Alec had to remain in the hut until all the vermin were gone from his body. After being in there a while he went out another door, and stood there completely naked for all the world to see (well, all of St Omer) as he was issued with a completely new set of clothes — uniform, socks, underwear, the lot — and new kit. And even then he still had a few of the little buggers on him. He had just embarked on a cycle that would go on for his entire time at the Western Front, one he would eventually just accept: dugouts — vermin — steam — new clothes — dugouts — vermin — steam — new clothes. All his worldly wealth — his canvas kitbag and its contents — had to go into the steam room with him, including the pieces of propeller. Even the photograph of his mother was deloused.

Alec spent only a couple of days at St Omer before being sent up to the line again. The Royal Flying Corps men treated him like an outsider. These were very lonely days indeed. No other AFC wireless operators could be found there, evidently having been and gone or been farmed out to the squadrons direct from the Australian General Base Depot at Rouelles.

For Alec the remainder of August 1917 consisted of being sent up to the line, conducting shoots, being shelled, receiving shrapnel wounds, getting lousy, getting attached to various squadrons of the RFC, returning to St Omer, and being pattern-bombed from the air. In mid-August he was attached to a Canadian artillery battery and saw action out near Armentières during the stunt on Hill 70. Weather conditions were most unfavourable. At least he enjoyed serving with the Canadians. He found them much more easygoing than the Pommies — which is not at all to say that he didn't like the Tommies, as he loved their tenacity and vigour — and got along with them well. The last few days of August, beset as they were by heavy rain and strong winds (this was meant to be summer!), were particularly miserable. Sometimes Alec would return to St Omer to find that his bed had been taken by someone else. The justification for this was that he was a Flying Corps wireless operator serving with the artillery, and blokes who spent half their life above the height of a trench parapet or a dugout roof, laying white strips of canvas out in the open, weren't exactly expected to return to their beds. The result was that he would be billeted in some farmhouse in a nearby village, away from the smell of boot polish.

There was one village in particular in which Alec spent quite a few days, thanks in no small part to the fact that thick fog prevented any art-obs. He and an English bloke found themselves as 'pals' in what wasn't so much a 'billet' as a fair dinkum private house. Here there was always a pot of coffee on the stove, always consumed strong, and always black.

There was very little to do except to walk through the village and have every woman say 'Bonjour, Monsieur' to them, and for the boys to reply 'Bonshor, Mamzelle'. They certainly didn't communicate very much with the villagers, except to say 'Bonshor', 'Bonswor', 'Commont allay vou' or 'Parlay vou onglay?' They were the only young men in the entire village. The population consisted only of old people, girls and very young boys. It was very quiet, the village was almost deserted. Nor was it the most hygienic of places, with no sewerage to speak of and farm animals roaming the streets.

Alec's English pal decided to 'decorate' the bedroom with pictures of girls. Alec wasn't particularly interested, because a letter from Effie Melville had been waiting at the Depot for him. He spent days reading it over and over again, agonising over the fact that no matter how many things he wanted to tell her — about him, about how rotten it was in the line, and how much he was missing her cousin Bob — all he could do was cross out every sentence on a Field Service Post Card except for the one reading 'I am well'. It was even forbidden to put the Os and Xs of hugs and kisses on these cards, lest it be construed as some sort of secret enemy code — there were certainly plenty of rumours about that spies and saboteurs were operating in the vicinity of St Omer. It was the same type of card that Alec was 'requested' to fill out each time before he went out to a battery. 'I am well' was the only sentence to remain not crossed out. That was the regulation and the cards were checked before dispatch. Alec could not understand why they were called postcards because there were no pictures on them. Considering the scenes he had seen up in the line, he reckoned this was probably just as well.

While waiting for the weather to clear he made a tiny electric motor. It was so small that he mounted it on a threepenny piece. A newspaper article was later written about it and another bloke given the credit, but it was Alec's invention and he kept the plans. The shaft of the motor was a sewing needle (which he took from his military-issue sewing kit, 'the Housewife') and the outside casing was a nut. While an ordinary DC motor must have a commutator, instead of having the wire of the armature wound down and back into the commutator, Alec had it glued onto the outside of the sewing needle and then back again. The motor was too small to be used for anything practical. Alec invented it just for the pleasure of it, and to prove that it could be done. For power he used a torch battery; later versions used the six-volt battery from the wireless set. These versions didn't last more than half a minute, but just having them run was an achievement. Alec Griffiths had constructed something of worth in a world of worthless destruction.

Before long he was delivered by Crossley tender to another artillery battery. The tender, a sort of general-purpose vehicle used for anything including taking scared young wireless operators to the line and bringing dead pilots back to the squadron, was a clumsy-looking thing that would have seemed more at home delivering fruit to a greengrocer's in London. Nonetheless, it was a hardy old bus, despite the fact that it could only go a certain way off-road before Alec had to get out and walk. His instructions were simple: Follow the duckboards. Judging by the ruined equipment and the occasional wrecked howitzer lying in the mud, there was no other choice. Nearby, a horse had its two front legs and its nose half buried in the mud and seemed to be ready to kick the first poor bloke who passed behind it. As Alec edged closer, he realised there was no need to worry. Dead horses can't kick.

The stinking mud must have been at least a couple of feet deep. The few live horses he saw had to avoid the duckboards, because they'd easily lose their footing and slip through. The duckboards were sectioned in order that they could be lifted up and carried. They were double boards, like pallets, only much bigger. The idea behind this great advance over earlier 'technology' was that the mud would have to be very thin for it to slip through and sink the boards. This didn't prevent the mud from having a damn good try, though. In some places the duckboards had simply floated away like rafts cast adrift on a chocolate sea. In these places the going was especially difficult. By comparison, the foot-deep mud of the dairy farms Alec had worked on had been a desert. The mud was so treacly that his greatest battle at this time was with his own legs. Each time he tried to extricate his rearward leg from the tenacious goo, the effort would force his forward leg in deeper still. It was less a matter of walking over the ground than wading through it.

All the area around was a total wilderness. Besides the occasional stumpy trunk of a tree, a stranded gun or a pile of bricks left from a house, everything else was completely blown clear. There were no hiding places for snipers or machine-gunners or anyone else as dastardly. There was a terrible smell that permeated for miles around. Alec had a flashback to the times on the farm in New South Wales when a bull calf was born and he was tasked with killing it. If it wasn't used straight away, it would smell. That smell was not unlike the smell that hung thick in the air now. Corpses, and pieces of corpse, littered the ground.

* * *

His new battery was an English one. He introduced himself to the battery commander, a man with a handlebar moustache so stereotyped that he should have been a player in a theatrical performance. Alec was ordered to set up his equipment. He prepared and erected his aerial, which was directional and had to be faced away from the enemy. Within no time at all he could hear every wireless station around, because they were on an undamped frequency. There wasn't even continuous wave; it was just one big splosh. Alec knew this meant that every other receiver within cooee would soon be able to hear the signals from the RE8. Right now, the signals were coming out all garbled and meant nothing to him. He was listening to German signals — somewhere along the line, one of the friendly batteries was about to get a pounding. Alec closed his eyes momentarily. 'Please,' he said to no one. 'Please not ours.'

After informing the battery commander about the German signals Alec prepared his ground strips, settled down in the dugout, and waited. He thought about his school days. He also thought about how utterly irrelevant those days were out here. At school, no one had taught him how to tolerate vermin through his clothes. Nobody had taught him how to cope with the sight and stench of rotting corpses, nor the horrible gurgling sounds made by men who would soon join them. His teacher had never taught him the difference between high-explosive shells and shrapnel, or the differences between phosgene and chlorine.

School days were soon forgotten when Alec detected a strong signal, clearly stronger than any of the others. A plane was flying directly towards them. Some of the battery men made ready with their rifles, while others didn't seem to care. Alec wasn't too concerned; he had deciphered the signal and knew the plane was friendly. Friendly aeroplanes always flew directly towards the battery as the signal was much stronger than when they flew across.

Alec waited in the dugout for the shoot to commence, and thought about the dead horses. Some of the horses were used to move the guns up to different parts of the line, while others could be seen with 18-pounder shells strapped to their backs like saddles of brass. Alec wondered how these intelligent animals could see everything they saw — the filth, the death, the unspeakable everything — and still allow themselves to be taken up to the line time and time again. 'Then again, how could we?' he whispered. He had begun to talk to himself.

* * *

The weather was fining up as Alec was being taken back to the Depot at St Omer. For every pink young face he observed heading up to the battle zone, an ashen old face was heading back. The pink faces used one side of the road, the ashen ones the other. An invisible line divided them and Alec and his escort were driving down that line. He felt deeply for the pink-faced Tommies, for he knew they would be crossing that line in a matter of days, perhaps even hours.

At the Depot he was escorted straight to the steam room for delousing, and again given a completely new set of gear. As he was trying to find a bunk an NCO burst into his hut. 'Get yourself summat to eat and report for sentry duty,' he ordered. 'You've got fifteen minutes.' Alec drew a rifle from the armoury and reported to the guard commander, another surly NCO. Eating was pointless.

Alec loathed guard duty. It was soon pitch black, without any lights at the Depot whatsoever. The distant flash of unceasing gunfire was the only disruption to the darkness. To prevent saboteurs, guards were stationed all around the Depot, as they did at the aerodromes. The risk of sabotage was greater at the aerodromes than in St Omer, but the heads weren't taking any chances.

Not only was it pitch black, but it was bitterly cold too, even though it was September. Two hours on, four hours off. And you did it on your own. All Alec had was a rifle and a bayonet, and all the while he would be expecting a German at any minute to come up and bayonet him in the back, because he couldn't see a thing. He found the whole situation terrifying. The place was so foreign. Even the few winking stars looked strange. As he stood there, alone in the murky blackness, he wished that he could be looking up at the Southern Cross. Before long he realised, too, that he'd actually sooner be back in the dugouts.

That night, while Alec continued his guard duty alone, the No. 1 Aircraft Depot was hit by a devastating pattern-bombing raid. In many ways it was much worse than being shelled up in the line because it was so dark and it was impossible to see anything except for the flash of exploding bombs. Everyone knew there were German bombers above them, but they couldn't see them or try to avoid the bombs. Nor was it solely the Depot being hit. Alec was certain the Germans were trying to bomb the entire town of St Omer. He could do nothing but lie on the cold, damp ground and wait for it to be over.

Since the RE8 incident in England, and having been shelled up at the line, Alec was no longer really frightened of death — just the form in which it might come. And he didn't much like the idea of not seeing it coming, that night at the Depot. Yet he had to admit there were times when he was so tired and exhausted and had simply had enough that he'd welcome a 'Blighty one' — a wound that would not only take him back to England but take him out of hell.

The following morning revealed the consequences of the bombing raid. Craters littered the ground surrounding the buildings and huts had been destroyed. On the bush telegraph Alec heard that quite a few RFC chaps had been killed. He didn't get too much time to reflect on it, however. From out of nowhere an NCO approached Alec. 'Griffiths,' the sergeant said. 'Pack your kit. You're off to another squadron, but not until tomorrow morning. In the meantime, you've got one night's local leave.'

In the late afternoon Alec and a few Australian Flying Corps blokes who had recently come in from the line headed off to an estaminet some distance from St Omer. In lamplit comfort it wasn't hard for them to imagine that the muffled sound of artillery in the distance was nothing more than the crash of pounding surf on an Australian beach. They ordered 'poms de terz and erfs' in a medley of thick Australian accents, and were rewarded with plates of eggs and chips which they wolfed down in no time. They got talking to a few lads from other units too. Soon the room filled with calls of 'Donnay moy plus de vin blong.' And did the white wine flow that night! And the beer! But Alec, being a teetotaller, drank coffee.

The estaminet was run by a lovely middle-aged Frenchwoman and her three daughters. Photos of the men of the family, wearing the powder-blue military uniform of the French *poilus*, adorned the mantelpieces. You dared not enquire into their fate. This was the country, after all, that had suffered through Verdun.

A game of two-up, the dominant recreation for Australians on the Western Front, was being held outside. (Occasionally the Australians would play pitch and toss, using old horseshoes as quoits to be thrown at a stake in the ground. Cards weren't played very often. But two-up was played whenever the hint of a chance presented itself; that is, when there were enough men). All the currency was in small notes, French of course. You had to have a lot of notes to be able to lay claim to any quantity of money. Right now the 'wealthy' players were a bit scarce, as the wind was howling and money-hungry. Still, despite the wind there were a few blokes around the ring with stacks of money so high they had to put them on the ground and stand on them. The elected spinner tonight, as on all two-up nights, was a real larrikin. The boys considered this just as well, because the ring could get pretty rowdy.

Each time some bloke rang in the nob, the gathering would go wild. Someone joked that the brass should make a pre-battle game of two-up a compulsory parade. 'Seein' some bloke gettin' two heads in the spin would fire up the fellers far more than any trench whistle ever will, let me tell ya!' he said. 'Even better if we've all put wagers on before the stunt,' his mate remarked. A third man grinned at them. 'Yeah, but what's the point of winning so many onks before a stunt? Ya can't spend it when yer dead.'

It wasn't long before the Australians were singing 'Waltzing Matilda', 'One Two Three, Australian Boys Are We' (much to the chagrin of the handful of Tommies in their midst), and a version of 'Mademoiselle from Armentières' in which the mademoiselle hadn't been kissed for 40 years and in which, it seemed to Alec, every other verse ended in beers. They sang with all the abandon that only beers can elicit. Beers, that is, mixed with the knowledge that some of the boys were drinking the amber fluid for the last time. And although they weren't Pommies, the AFC lads sang 'Take me back to dear old Blighty, Blighty is the place for me'. Yet Alec didn't think there was much thought about fighting for Empire. Not among this lot and not among any other 'Empire troops' he had encountered. It was simply that you were in the service, and you had to do the job. Many Australians never really thought about who they were fighting for, other than themselves. Like Alec's their patriotism was very real, but it was for Australia, not Empire.

The important thing was that, by the end of the night, the Australian Flying Corps men had murdered almost every song in existence.

Alec was perhaps the only AFC man to wake the next morning *sans* hangover. He was taken to yet another aerodrome, to do whatever odd jobs they could find for him, as it was too foggy to conduct any artillery shoots. Although Flanders was approaching winter rather than leaving it, the weather was becoming better now, despite the few foggy days.

He was given a job in the workshop. With the scale of the war ever increasing, the aerodrome facilities on the Western Front had to be able to be moved in a hurry, as the line shifted frequently. Consequently the workshop was in a large lorry, complete with generator, drilling machine and lathe. Alec's job was to look after this engineer's shop; he liked it because it was what the English soldiers called a 'cushy job'.

There was a catch, however. The generator on the lorry also powered all the lights around the drome, and at night time it was Alec's job to shut the generator down at 'lights out'. This meant that he had to find his way to bed in the dark, which, after being caught in the night bombing raid at St Omer, he didn't like at all. He hit upon the idea of rigging up a Tickler's jam tin with just enough petrol in it to run the generator while he got to his bed. At that point the lights of the entire aerodrome would go out as if on cue.

The lads didn't always get to sleep immediately after lights out, though, due to noise. At this particular aerodrome night bombers were frequently sent out to bomb the enemy 20 or 30 miles away. When Alec heard them taking off, it always struck him how brave were the men who flew them. These aeroplanes — DH4s and Armstrong Whitworth FK8s — were flimsy contraptions, and they didn't have any wireless communication to tell them where they were. But reaching their targets by compass wasn't a problem. Getting back home and landing *in turn* without crashing — that was a problem.

The landing strip was set out with flares, each consisting of an oil drum full of waste cotton soaked in kero and set alight. They were strategically placed, with three on one side of the landing strip and one on the other. The pilot had always to keep the single flare on his left-hand side when landing. This wasn't too difficult. But knowing *when* to land — so they wouldn't all come in at once — was different.

Each pilot was supplied with a klaxon horn driven by a battery, and a Morse key. Each plane had a number assigned to it. When the pilots were coming home they would work their number on the Morse key (which was connected to the klaxon horn) so that the men at the drome could hear them. They could be heard for miles around, even across the line. The pilots didn't care if they were drawing the enemy's attention, the important thing was to get down. The ground crew would lie in their huts, laughing until they cried, as the returning bombers sounded for all the world like a flock of honking geese during the mating season.

From the three side flares, the pilots would know where the aerodrome was located. Then, if the no. 2 plane, say, came back, frantically sounding its no. 2 signal, the ground crew would light two special flares and the pilot would land. No other pilot was permitted to land until the number of flares corresponded to his assigned number. The flares were all the pilots had to assist them in landing. The only thing that saved them from crashing on the landing strip, which was nothing more than a paddock, was the fact that they were incapable of coming in to land any faster than they did.

* * *

A few days after the big German bombing raid on St Omer, Alec took off in an Armstrong Whitworth — a 'Big Ack' — heading for the line. Despite the fact that the line was beginning to dry out, the word around the traps had been that neither a Crossley tender nor a motorcycle was capable of getting him through to his next battery appointment fast enough. Alec had no desire to fly in a plane, but had no choice.

The sky looked beautiful from the aeroplane. The landscape did not — it was so grey that it looked to Alec like a photograph shot with his VPK camera. Of course, he did not have his camera with him, having left it behind in England. Had he been discovered with it he would have been in a world of strife, especially if it was a British officer who discovered it. Alec had heard that if a Tommy was caught with a camera in the field he could be shot. At the very least, he might be subjected to what they called Field Punishment No. 1. Under this punishment, the ankles and wrists of the offender were lashed to the wheel of a wagon or a howitzer, and he would be left there for days. Alec shuddered at the thought.

They landed in the middle of nowhere. The ground was on a slight rise. In the distance Alec could see observation balloons and knew instantly the direction in which the line lay. The crash of gunfire helped too. The ruins of some buildings a good way off were pointed out to him by the pilot, who said something, but all Alec could hear above the din of the aeroplane's engine was the noise of guns.

Laden with his equipment, he dismounted from the plane and trudged off in the general direction of the ruins as the Big Ack ran up to fly back to the drome. He felt very much alone. The scene that confronted him was nothing short of desolate. It was easy to keep his bearings on the ruins, there was very little else around to distract him.

A few hundred yards further on he came across the wreck of a British fighter. How long had it been there? It could have been two days, it could have been two years. A chap at the drome had told him that the area in which he now was had been fought over in 1914 and again in 1915. To Alec it looked as though it had been fought over in *1419*, and all the years since. They were a frequent sight along the line, these wrecked planes. If they came down near a squadron a rescue crew would be dispatched. Otherwise they were abandoned. The main item to disappear from the wrecks was the pilot's watch. It was considered the most worthwhile souvenir, by both sides. Another favourite souvenir was the compass, carried by some of the machines. Alec surveyed the mangled mess in front of him. He made to look in it, but his thoughts returned involuntarily to the RE8 accident back in England. He turned away and walked on.

Shortly he came to some shell craters filled with putrid green water, in which there were bits of animals, men and machines. The craters looked like bowls of soup. Many wounded men had died in them because they hadn't the strength to pull themselves out. Alec recalled the pledge made by some wretched Australian politician to support England 'to our last man and our last shilling', and felt sick.

At length he arrived at a battery. Was it the right one? He wasn't sure, but the battery commander claimed that they were expecting a wireless operator, and needed one quick smart. He didn't care who it was. He literally stumbled across the dugout. He hadn't seen it due to it being so well camouflaged. Once again he set up his equipment and settled down to wait. A sergeant entered the dugout. He was short and wiry, foul with mud, and his angular cheekbones shone in the half-light of the kerosene lantern. Something about him was reticent and wistful, but Alec couldn't put a name to it. Watchful, the sergeant seemed to be waiting for the battery commander and the other men in the dugout to acknowledge him. He then collapsed in a heap on the floor, exhausted.

The waiting lasted a few hours, and Alec managed to get quite a lot of woodcarving done on the handle of his walking stick. He also made the acquaintance of a handful of the gunners. They were a friendly mob. A lot of activity filled the air and, with the exception of a few brave RFC lads, most of it seemed to be German. In any event, it gave Alec something to watch. He figured that there wouldn't be too many Allied observation machines in the air now, since they were a favourite prey of the German fighters. In the earlier stages of the war, German aeroplanes would come along from behind and have no trouble in shooting down the Allies' observation machines. Later, the observers were provided with a machine-gun, which faced backwards. This proved to be a good — though not at all impregnable — defence against German aerial attack, but it also meant that the pilot not only had to fly the plane, but he also had to conduct the artillery observation and wireless signalling as well.

* * *

After the shoot Alec found himself watching what they called 'the circus'. He had no idea why they called it that; perhaps it was because the aerial dogfights were so entertaining to the troops on the ground. The gunners loved them. Provided there were no shells dropping, you could watch a dogfight in the distance and be in little or no danger. One of the gunners suggested they bet on the outcome. 'Twenny onks says the Hun loses,' came the wager call. 'Twenty says he doesn't.' 'I'm in!' 'Right-oh, bet yer twenty onks he doesn't.' Alec was not a gambling man and simply sat there, gazing up at the watercolour sky, fascinated by the fighter planes ducking and weaving. He remembered the young pilots in England, many of whom he had taught the Morse code, being so keen to get over to the Western Front and 'get a Hun'. And Alec knew that it was the undoing of a lot of them. These young pilots were so keen that they could be easily led into the traps set for them by the Germans. Yet even when they saw their mates brought back dead in a Crossley tender their first and only desire was to get a Hun. Only then would they be seen by their fellow pilots as gallant. Most of them were no more than 19 or 20 years old. Now, in the dogfight in front of Alec, there were pilots who might never make it to their 21st birthday. They seemed intent on ensuring they never would.

CHAPTER TWELVE
Anywhere But Here

The air battle died down. Alec had seen a couple of machines spiral into the ground. They'd crashed into a forest that wasn't really a forest at all, just a series of upright posts. As he looked away from the plumes of smoke rising into the air, he was taken aback at the sight of dozens of German prisoners being escorted from the track off to the right of the battery and into his area. The prisoners weren't what he had expected, somehow. They looked, well, normal. Not much different from the gunners. The main difference was that quite a number of the Germans sported the distinctive black and white flash of the Iron Cross. Most of them were just boys, with a handful of older soldiers with greying hair and beards. Their faces didn't look dastardly or evil. Just scared. They were probably thinking the same thing as they looked at Alec.

At the dugout — no more than a sandbagged trench with a corrugated-iron lid on it — the smell of food filled his nostrils, and Alec realised that he hadn't eaten since morning. Failing to find any spare food in the dugout, he filled his water canteen from a tin in the corner and drank. The water tasted like the smell of petrol. As he spat it out, a bombardier who had been watching him laughed.

'What's up, young feller? You don't like our water?'

'It's fine. It just tastes like petrol,' Alec replied.

'That's because it's brought up to us in petrol cans ... if it's brought up at all.'

The taste of the water, though repugnant, was irrelevant. They had no choice but to drink from the petrol can. Ironically, they were surrounded by water but couldn't drink it. To have drunk from the watercourses would have led to serious illness or death, for the water was contaminated not only by the corpses in it, but also by gas shells.

Alec was, however, exceptionally hungry. 'Would it be possible to get something to eat, Bom?' he ventured.

The bombardier looked at Alec thoughtfully. 'You're new to this part of the line, aren't you?' Alec nodded. 'Well, we've just taken a bunch of prisoners off the hands of one of the battalions, and you can always tell when there's been a bunch of prisoners taken, 'cos we have to go short on food. They get some of our food, and of course' — he glanced to his right, as if to consult with someone, but there was nobody nearby — 'we've been taking a fair few prisoners these last few days.' Alec nodded again. 'Here, have one of mine.' The bombardier handed Alec a tin of bully beef, producing it as if from nowhere. The bombardier, Alec later learned, was nicknamed 'the Magician'.

Alec sat himself on a wooden box, opened the tin with his jackknife, and ate. It wasn't until he had half finished that he realised he was up to the top of his puttees in mud and water. Some of the dugout floor was awash, while other parts had dried out in recent days, like the ground outside. Alec had learned a little about 'trench feet' and knew that the condition was caused by your feet being continuously wet. Careful to ensure that he didn't lose his boots, he extracted his feet from the slush and shifted to a drier spot.

During the ensuing days the battery conducted many more shoots. They fired a great many shells at the Hun, and he fired a great deal more back at them. A fair proportion of these were gas shells, along with high-explosive ordnance for a more devastating effect. The gas shells were easy to detect, even before you smelt the phosgene. They went off with a pop rather than a loud explosion. Gas masks were often donned before anyone had the chance to sound the gas gong. The masks fogged your vision and this, plus the fact that they were physically hindering and made breathing awkward, meant that your job became more difficult.

Not every gunner managed to get his 'gaspirator' on in time. Casualties from gas were commonplace in this area and the main problem was getting the victims out of the line. Even the very worst cases seldom got to an advanced dressing Station straight away — let alone a casualty clearing station — and might then have to wait quite some time before receiving medical attention. Every man in the battery had his job to do, upon which many other lives depended. They helped the casualties when they could but sometimes, during a shoot, they simply could not help.

When Alec wasn't working, and there were no casualties, he just sat in the dugout and wished the sound of gunfire and the incessant shell explosions would go away. All he wanted to do was get back to the Depot in St Omer and read Effie's letters (which he knew would be waiting for him) and see if there was any news of Bob Lauchland. They were bound to run into each other eventually, he reckoned, since St Omer was the sort of base to which all the wireless operators would at one time or another have to go.

But things along the line started to hot up. There was now more gunfire than Alec had ever experienced. Hundreds of guns were firing thousands of shells. All manner of guns were being transported. The men at the battery were starting to talk. Were they hitting the usual road junctions? Or were they hitting observation posts, other batteries, German troops? Furphies that spoke of a big push spread quickly, for it had been relatively quiet for a while before these last few days, and suddenly a lot was happening. Alec was not told anything by the battery commander except that he would not be permitted to return to his current squadron, or indeed any other squadron, because he 'might be needed again' in the next couple of days.

Nightly Alec heard — felt — the shells explode. Nightly he heard the screams of mangled men. He heard the German night bombers flying over on their way to bomb the Allies' rear areas. He heard the other blokes in the cramped dugout scratching themselves. He fought his own private war against the chats that infested his singlet and flannel shirt. And each night he wished he was anywhere but here.

It was the same during the day too, especially the day when a huge bombardment began. It seemed as if every Allied gun on the Western Front was firing, and soon afterwards Alec was sure that every German gun was replying. Acrid smoke from the guns filled the air. It was so thick that Alec could taste its bitterness on his tongue. He could hear shells landing around the battery. A couple landed so close to the dugout that pieces of them whacked into the side of the gas alarm — an old 18-pounder shell casing hanging at the entrance — and dirt and debris was flung into the dugout. The artillerymen whose dugout Alec was sharing scarcely noticed. 'At least they're not bloody five-point-nines,' one of them said drily. More landed very close to the dugout, shaking the earth each time and sending no longer fear but despair through Alec.

Sporadic shelling went on for a few days. During this time Alec was used both by his present battery and by another one for more shoots. In September 1917 it was hard to remember what day it was, let alone which battery you were with and what targets they were hitting. Alec just knew that things were leading up to something big.

The rain began again the night they started the 'something big'. There were all sorts of movement along the line, but nobody informed Alec what was going on. Incendiary shells were occasionally sent their way by the German artillery, briefly turning night into day. Eerily, these shells seemed to illuminate helmets more than anything else. They lit up not only the helmets worn by the gunners but also the helmets strewn across the surrounding ground, helmets covering the skulls of the fallen.

When the heavy barrages started — both Allied and German — just before dawn, it became apparent to Alec that there was indeed a big attack going on. Shells began to land very close and in quite some volume, as if the Germans were specifically trying to target Alec's battery. Perhaps they were. Nothing could be seen except with the assistance of the flickering guns as they fired, or the flash of incoming shells. Alec's eyes never became accustomed to the murky gloom, for it was never completely dark long enough to achieve night vision. And the images of shell flash remained imprinted on his retina for what seemed an eternity.

A man kept running in and out of the dugout, reporting on Gunner Smith having been hit and wounded or Gunner Jones copping it or coming a gutser. Alec was thankful that he was in the dugout and not up top having to do his job. The thankfulness didn't last. The whole area was blanketed in wet mist as daylight arrived, but above the sound of constant gunfire he heard the unmistakable drone of RE8s flying over the line from the rear. Alec felt sure that no art-obs could be conducted in this weather, despite the fact that the battery commander now briefed him to be ready.

'The RFC are up top scouting around for any signs of a German counterattack, and will be directing artillery fire where necessary. Machine-gun posts are to be singled out for special treatment. There'll also be counter-battery work directed at batteries within range of our guns.'

Alec wasn't sure he needed to know all this to do his job, but said 'Yes, sir' anyway.

When the mist began to clear a couple of hours later, he knew he'd be earning his eight shillings. He could scarcely believe the scene around him when he emerged from the dugout. Somehow Fritz had created more shell holes where there had simply been no more room for them. And still his shells were falling. Great spouts of water shot into the air each time a dud landed in a crater. Dead men littered the area around the battery, nothing but bundles of rags.

Fortunately, with no sign of German observation machines in the air, the incoming shells were anything but accurate. The first call for fire came not long after Alec had set up his crystal receiver and antenna again. He received the signal F-A-N, which meant that an Allied pilot had spotted some enemy infantry. The pilot gave the location of the target, and Alec raced into the dugout to inform the battery commander. He noticed that the battery commander had marked a spot near a place with a strange name beginning with Z, and began drawing a clock face centred on it. Alec ran back outside, his head full of the colours — reds, blues, greens — that he had seen on the map. They were the only colours he had seen for days. All else had been grey, black or dirty brown, or the ridiculous white of his six-foot by eighteen-inch canvas signalling strips.

The shoot commenced, and Alec's world once again became one of wireless messages, gunfire, laying out strips of canvas in the open among the shell holes, Hun shells exploding nearby, and a lot of running. The rate of fire of the 18-pounders became particularly intense.

The day grew clear as the sun emerged from the now rapidly dissipating mist. The battery spent all morning firing the guns at everything from enemy posts to observation balloons. At one stage, Alec received a message from an RE8 that deciphered to 'I can see some infantry.' The pilot was quite skilled at sending the message, but Alec reckoned he must have been either very inexperienced or very nervy, because the proper signal should have been the simple F-A-N. Alec managed a smile, his first for some time; F-A-N would have been much easier for the pilot to tap out.

During another shoot, the battery was attacked by a German aeroplane — the first Alec had seen for the day — and a handful of gunners were wounded by machine-gun fire. The scattered artillery shells continued to fall for much of the day, but to little effect. At one stage the gas gong was rung and Alec had to continue his job wearing his gas mask. Running out into the open to arrange the canvas strips, and dashing back again, was not easy while in that accursed mask.

As the sun was setting, a rosy glow spread over the battlefield. Then, as the sun finally slipped into the dust and mud, the glow intensified to the golden red of embers in a dying fire. Alec looked at it and wanted to cry. How could such beauty exist amid such horror? At nightfall, after one final bout of gunfire, things became quiet, except for the tinkle of harnesses as more guns were brought into position not far away. Northern stars perplexed southern eyes once more. When Alec was finally stood down he ate his first meal of the day. He had been so scared up top during the shelling and the plane attack that, once again, he had not noticed how hungry he was. He was deeply tired, the sound of shells lingering in his ears. The moment he lay down on his sodden groundsheet he fell asleep and dreamt the sweet dream of being taken, wounded, out of the line.

* * *

Alec woke to the rolling thunder of artillery. Near? Far? He couldn't tell. It continued intermittently but with great ferocity for a few hours after dawn. He sat in the slush of the dugout and carved the shape of a hand into the walking stick he was making, waiting for the noise and the smell to go away. But the latter wasn't going anywhere. The foul air was laden with the stench of decomposing animals and people, and was blended with the curious aroma of the creosol used to try and get rid of the flies, and the kerosene all soldiers used to try and rid themselves of the vermin.

He didn't know what made him carve the shape of a man's hand. He had seen so many hands of dead men sticking up from the ground in the past few weeks that it should have been the last thing he would think of carving. Those hands reaching upwards haunted him. Reaching for what?

His dream of getting out of the line came suddenly true. There was the sound of a motorbike and Alec hurriedly prepared his equipment for departure.

He recognised little of what he saw as they headed westwards. Perhaps he had never been here before. Or perhaps he had, perhaps it had been transformed in a matter of days. Most of the roads they rode on had been shelled out of existence. Eventually they got on to a plank road, parts of which were damaged by shellfire.

Occasionally they saw a couple of stretcher-bearers walking towards the road with wounded men. Once or twice they saw groups of them — almost enough to start a 'stretcher-bearer platoon'. Some of the bearers were lucky, as their burden was light. Daisy-clippers, the shells that sent fragments flying horizontally just above ground level, had seen to that. Men who had had their legs cut away from beneath them were a light burden indeed for the stretcher-bearers. Other victims of daisy-clippers, who had been crouching when the shells detonated, were left where they had fallen. If a man was caught in this position, the daisy-clipper fragments often became his guillotine.

Along the edge of the road Alec saw not one or two dead horses but entire teams, most of them disembowelled and with other hideous wounds. The guns and limbers they had been hauling, to which they were still hitched, seemed to mock them from their muddy resting place. An occasional shell landed near the motorcycle on the way but Alec scarcely noticed.

Back at St Omer, he was ordered to delouse and to be ready to move at a moment's notice. He went through the long steam hut and was issued at the end with a new uniform and kit. He felt clean. Better still, there were letters from Effie to be devoured.

Her words came from a different world. A more human world, a world where people still went for evening walks, and had Sunday dinner together at the family table in the middle of the day. A world where a shell was something to be marvelled at during a stroll along the beach, not a loathsome object that hurled through the air and brought with it death. How he yearned for that world! How he yearned to meet this Effie.

Scarcely had he finished reading about how 'more and more each day' she wanted to meet him when a large number of aeroplanes landed, one at a time. Never before had Alec seen so many planes in the air around an aerodrome at the one time. These DH5s belonged to No. 68 Squadron RFC (the Australian squadron that would later be redesignated No. 2 Squadron AFC) under the command of Major Ozzie Watt and were freshly in from England.

Alec felt proud to be Australian as he watched Ozzie Watt — about whom he had heard so much praise — and the other Aussie pilots coming in to land. But even before the pilots had dismounted from their machines, he was ordered over to a waiting RE8. He was being attached to No. 69 Squadron RFC.

Being attached to another squadron didn't mean very much. Alec had already been 'attached' to half a dozen of them, and at least twice as many artillery batteries. Not once had any paperwork been done (not any that he saw) about these attachments and detachments. He thought that perhaps he, like many other AFC wireless operators, was being moved around too fast and at too short a notice for the paperwork to catch up with him. Perhaps no one in the AFC or the RFC really knew which batteries he was being sent to, or even cared. But 'attached' he had to be because he had to be given a home somewhere, however briefly.

Alec was dropped off at his latest home, the 69th, at an aerodrome near Savy, between Arras and St Pol. It was 21 September 1917. The day before had been an important day. Hundreds of thousands of shells from more than a thousand howitzers and guns had been fired by the Allies against the Germans in the Battle of Menin Road Ridge, and Alec had played a part in it. More significantly for him, it was exactly one year to the day since he had enlisted at Marrickville Town Hall as a boy of sixteen. Alec felt as though he had aged ten years, not one. Again his thoughts turned to Bob Lauchland, as he crossed his fingers in the hope that Bob just might be there at the 69th.

CHAPTER THIRTEEN
A Lone Red Flower

Marrickville Town Hall seemed so very far away. Around him now, as the light faded, RE8s littered the aerodrome. Alec certainly felt as if this was home. No. 69 Squadron RFC was in fact No. 3 Squadron, Australian Flying Corps, though many people persisted in calling it the 69th.

He didn't stay at the 69th Squadron drome for very long, but he did go down to the line in a plane to a sector a fair distance away to do a shoot where there was an important job going down, in a sector a fair distance away. As with all such flights, Alec was to be the navigator on the plane. 'Fly on bearing ... for fifteen minutes, then land in a field between a fosse and a windmill,' the major ordered.

'Sir? What's a fosse?' Alec asked.

'It's ... errr ... it's ...' The major turned to a nearby sergeant. 'What's a fosse, Sergeant?'

'A disused coal mine, sir!'

The officer turned back to Alec. 'It's a disused coal mine.'

'Thank you sir,' replied Alec, as he mounted the aeroplane and settled in with his weighty equipment. The pilot was a fellow by the name of Henry Wrigley, and he was either a lieutenant or a captain. As he was preparing to run up, he said to Alec, 'Let's go searching for Huns! We'll see if we can get ourselves a Hun on the way down.'

Alec didn't particularly want to encounter any Huns on the way down, but he couldn't tell Wrigley this. 'Can you use that thing?' Wrigley asked, nodding at the Lewis machine-gun mounted on a ring around the cupola.

'If I have to, sir,' Alec replied.

'That's the spirit, blue!' Wrigley said, and they were on their way.

Although Alec was trained on the Lewis gun at his disposal, he was not at all sorry when their search proved fruitless. They could feel the concussion from the shells exploding along the line, jolting the RE8 up and down with the burst of each shell. In a strange way, Alec found the shells bursting around them quite a thrill. The plane seemed to float just like a piece of paper getting blown around by the explosions.

Wrigley made three abortive landings before they finally got down. Their landing strip was an open paddock — prepared airstrips were pointless because the line was moving so often. A rough landing on rougher ground shook both occupants, and Alec felt sure the only thing that saved them was that they weren't doing excessive speeds. Wrigley turned around to him, smiled, and apologised. To the right and left, the line stretched as far as the eye could see. The occasional shell landed haphazardly near Alec and Wrigley, doing little more than add another hole to the thousands that already lay before them.

Wrigley took to the sky again. Alec gathered his equipment and made his way towards a gun battery in the open. No attempt had been made to camouflage it. He had serious doubts as to whether there was anything in the vicinity that could have been used for camouflage anyway. There were so many shell holes that they practically merged into one another. In one, an arm protruded from the side of the hole. In another, a heap of clothing and equipment lay in a heap at the bottom. On second glance, he realised the heap was a headless corpse. He did not allow himself a third glance.

Despite their surroundings the men at the battery were in reasonably cheery spirits. 'Don't worry about the feller you saw in that crump hole,' said one of the gunners to Alec. 'He doesn't disturb us. He's been there for weeks now and he never says a word.'

'What's it been like here?' enquired Alec sceptically.

There was no answer. He set up his equipment and sat around for only a few minutes shooing away flies until the shoot commenced. There was the subtle smell of decaying corpses in the air, and he would be pleased to do the job he had been sent to do and clear off.

A reasonably straightforward shoot was executed. The target most secret was a German troop train. In some distant headquarters, the rosellas had decided to risk a good pilot and a very scarce wireless operator, not to mention an aeroplane to get him on the spot to get the job done. Alec figured therefore that what had been destroyed — or at least what the battery had tried to destroy — must have been important. Certainly the fact that each gun had fired at least 30 shells drumfire spoke to the target's importance. Many stripped to the waist, the gunners had worked like the blazes. The guns themselves had sunk visibly deeper into the ground.

Alec heard the sound of a motorcycle engine. Just in time. The previously subtle smell was now becoming unbearable.

* * *

Back at the aerodrome, Alec spent the next few days repairing wireless equipment. He was now classed as an operator/mechanic, which means he was often called upon to do this work. Some of it arose because the pilots often landed without pulling in their weighted 100-foot copper wire aerial. These incidents would have been amusing had the damage not been so serious. By the time the aerial had been broken free it was all a terrific mess. Alec suspected it was just too much trouble for the pilots to wind in the aerial before landing, and so they 'forgot'. It was left to the poor air mechanics to fix up. The pilots didn't see that as a problem — the air mechanics had to be kept busy somehow, by Jove.

In the space of a few more days Alec was transferred to another location, and then another. His head swam in a whirlwind of change. During the interminable night of the 25th Alec heard aeroplanes directly above his new battery. Their beat sounded like that of the night bombers he had grown used to, and he speculated as to what their targets might be. There was definitely something doing.

He was awakened from his light sleep and was briefed by the battery commander. Yes, there was something doing all right. Alec was to set up his equipment and 'expect a busy day'. He knew it would be a long one too, for it had not even become light. He couldn't see much as dawn broke, but he sensed there was a lot going on. Word was there were even Allied infantry abreast of the battery area, so close to the front line was the battery.

Even once dawn pushed night away, a thick fog cloaked the Flanders landscape. Alec reckoned this made up for the last few days, which had been pretty fine. Scarcely anything could be seen. Alec could only just make out the guns of the battery. He couldn't see much, but he certainly heard. He heard what seemed like all the guns of the Western Front erupt at once. The noise of the shellfire was at once horrifying and awe-inspiring. Each side of the entire line seemed to be engaged in doing something to the other, and it wasn't long before Alec heard aeroplanes approaching. He had found on many occasions that the only way he could stay awake was to chew the inside of his mouth. Now, with the ear-splitting noise, there was no need.

The first call for artillery arrived not long after it grew light, though how the observers could actually see anything perplexed Alec. The clouds were as low as they were menacing. Most of Alec's work came around late morning, when the sun finally emerged. Thereafter the RFC pilots were able to observe much more enemy activity, and the battery was able to deal with it accordingly.

Alec had no idea what was going on in the attacks; only that his battery was called upon to fire at everything from German batteries to individual machine-guns, and that the entire length of the line at one stage was completely enveloped in smoke from the shelling. There was seldom any silence, so one grew used to the noise after a while.

He was particularly busy in the afternoon, when almost every transmission he received seemed to include F-A-N, the infantry of German counter-attacks. The men of the battery took quite a bit of shelling themselves, but it was far from the worst Alec had encountered, despite the fact that a piece of shrapnel gouged out a piece of his neck during one of the shoots.

The wound hurt like blazes, but he could do nothing but ignore it and continue with his job. By the time he could actually do something about the wound, there was nothing but a dull pain and a lot of dried blood. Once the fighting moderated he was more concerned with eating a decent meal, preferably warm. It had been brief, his part in the Battle for Polygoneveld, or Polygon Wood. But it had been, as the battery commander had warned, a very busy time.

The next few days saw Alec being sent to various batteries along the line. Activity had become relatively 'quiet' along the line. Nevertheless art-obs continued, it seemed, every day. He managed to get a lot of carving done, in between shoots. The Germans continued to attack, in relatively small doses, right through to the end of September. The fogs usually cleared by late morning, and Alec's afternoons were spent relaying target information to sundry battery commanders, laying out his strips on the mud, and being half-buried by the very same mud each time a shell landed nearby.

In the days following Polygoneveld, occasionally there'd be a spare man in the battery who would lay out the ground strips for him when he was too busy on the wireless, but in most cases every man had his own job to do so it was up to Alec. He was lucky with a couple of shoots when he was working with a particularly experienced pilot. You could tell when there was a very experienced pilot up top, because he wouldn't need to wait for the strips to go right out. If he saw them going out, that would be enough and he'd be satisfied. With experience, instead of waiting for the letter to go right out they could ascertain what letter it was intended to be, and the wireless operators would get the OK. Alec was most thankful for this, since it meant less exposure to German shells.

On the first of October he was sent back past Zillebeke and Ypres to the rear and given a couple of days' respite from the line. In many ways, getting leave was good. In other ways all it really amounted to was a break from the misery before that made the misery afterwards even more miserable. The sojourn at the rear at least gave you the opportunity to get 'clean' again, to feel like a human being.

Alec now noticed things he had never noticed before. Some Australians who had a sense of humour had written all sorts of words and messages on destroyed buildings. One notice read: 'The Manly ferry leaves from this corner'. Another, on a building standing next to a large lake, claimed this was Circular Quay. He smiled, then thought about his family in Sydney and wondered what they were up to. How Lock and Fred were doing on their ships, if they were still alive.

Pondering this he headed off to a local estaminet with a few other Flying Corps blokes. Like the other boozers, this place wasn't run by the services, it was run privately.

Wherever there were no estaminets there'd usually be something run by the Salvation Army, the Church Army or the Red Cross, where the soldiers could go for something to eat and drink. Yes, the Salvos did a great job. Wherever the troops were likely to be, whether or not they were billeted there, there was always some arrangement for a little bit of 'society' in that vicinity. There would be a great congregation at the estaminets in particular, and this one was no exception. Alec ordered 'poms de terz' and wolfed them down as if they were his first meal in weeks. They made a tremendous change from bully, pork and beans, biscuits and jam, and Maconochies.

Back at another squadron, a bundle of letters awaited Alec. There was one from his mother, with bits and pieces of family news but nothing about his brothers, but most of the letters were from Effie. Alec reckoned she must have been writing a few times a week. In most cases, all Alec could write in return was 'I am quite well'. The occasions on which he was permitted to write more than a few words had been rare indeed. In every letter she would ask about Bob, since she hadn't heard from him. Alec wanted to write to her and explain that he hadn't heard from Bob either, and that at any given time he could have been located twenty miles from him or as little as 200 yards, without either of them knowing it. But that information would have been censored.

Out in the line, water was everywhere. So were observation balloons. Alec had seen plenty of the balloons earlier, tethered by anchors to the torn earth. Frequently German pilots appeared from nowhere and machine-gunned them; the observers had to jump clear wearing a parachute. Not many people volunteered for the Balloon Corps.

* * *

The battery was located in what only a few days before had been no man's land. It was easy for Alec to tell that because there were so few fresh shell craters. No man's land was the safest area of all from the ravages of shelling, since it was too close to the forward trenches of both sides for it to be shelled often. Of course the line moved backwards and forwards; some areas had changed hands fifteen times. Alec had much in common with the line, moving backwards, forwards, backwards, forwards, sideways — never staying in one place long enough to make any friends. And the ones he had, he never saw. Now he settled in as best he could at the makeshift dugout, which looked like an old gun emplacement. Not even a tin roof graced the haphazard structure. Men were scrounging anything they could to build one, but no matter how hard they tried it would remain a big, wet windy hole in the ground.

The battery commander, a man of less than 25, briefed Alec on what he would be required to do the next day. Where there should have been a major's rank on the battery commander's shoulders were the pips of a lieutenant. The artillery of all the armies on the Western Front were running short of men. Furphies back at the estaminets were rife that some batteries were suffering a 100 per cent casualty rate every week or so. Seeing a young subaltern as battery commander gave weight to the rumours.

Alec settled in to 'sleep' in the spongy mess that was the floor of the dugout. An occasional flare illuminated the blackness, serving only as an open invitation for both sides to start shelling each other even more than usual. He would always try and sleep at night. But usually, the guns and planes were interested in allowing no such thing. Tonight, after each spate of shells had landed nearby throughout the night, Alec rolled over and tried to get back to 'sleep'. Each time he was woken he was thankful that the darkness made it almost impossible to see what was going on along the line. What he could feel was bad enough. He awoke a couple of hours before dawn, lonely and shivering. He couldn't see anybody else. For company he had his gas respirator, shell dressing, kitbag, wireless and blanket. His blanket was soaked through from rain and from groundwater seeping into the dugout. His Flying Corps greatcoat was hopelessly inadequate. An Army greatcoat, which weighed six or seven pounds when dry, could weigh as much as 30 pounds when soaking wet, but at least it reached down below your leggings. The AFC version didn't even reach your knees, and Alec's knees were frozen. It looked very dapper on a parade ground on a dry day, but was useless when trying to warm your legs in the bottom of a muddy hole.

Despite his teeth chattering, Alec managed to snatch a few more minutes, sleep before being woken to the pleasant surprise that his home now had a roof. This was fortunate, for the drizzle of the previous day had become rain. He had something to eat in the dark and did his best to shave and to clean his equipment. The instant it was light he would have to set the gear up. Around him the dull sound of brushes against metal spoke of guns being cleaned. A great barrage thundered in the distance as it grew light, almost in reply to the German shelling that had been coming the way of the battery for some time. For the next few hours a lot of fighting went on up and down the line, but Alec didn't think he would be out there doing his job because the clouds were hanging low in the sky like fluffy grey half-deflated balloons. Too low, he reckoned, for any art-obs. He shivered violently from the cold.

No matter how hard he tried, he couldn't stop. An image of walking barefoot through warm cow dung entered his head, and he allowed himself a teeth-chattering smile.

Around mid-morning a number of German prisoners arrived, followed by a torrent of German shells. Being shelled was akin to having a compound interest loan. The first repayment was a dreadful inconvenience. Each subsequent instalment was progressively more horrific. You never grew used to it, really. You just accepted that you were in debt, and that the shells would continue to fall. The men of the battery shared their rations with the prisoners and then shook hands. The whole thing struck Alec as silly. For the rest of the day, having been proved wrong about the clouds, he was kept busy with calls for fire, the targets ranging from infantry to German artillery batteries. Laying out the canvas strips was difficult in the high winds, and with shrapnel whirring above his head he wanted to give up. He knew he couldn't. In such circumstances you just had to knuckle down and get on with the job. Fortunately the pilots of the observation machines were experienced and didn't appear to rely on the signal strips much anyhow.

In Alec's battery most of the guns were buried in mud up to the cradle; one was even buried to within four inches of its elevated muzzle. The guns stood as steel monuments on muddy islands, surrounded by an ocean of shell holes. The gunners, though shattered in nerve, continued to serve. Occasionally, they would go to ground. You knew things were pretty serious when gunners went to ground. And casualties mounted and the guns were served by fewer and fewer men.

The time came for Alec to leave the battery. 'Where's the duckboard track?' he asked one of the gunners. The local landscape had been so transformed he found it difficult to gain his bearings. 'Just wait for a plonker to come in, Griffo, and you'll soon see where it is,' the gunner replied, two fingers and a thumb outstretched in the gesture of 'It's over there somewhere.' Alec kept an eye on the general direction indicated. A couple of minutes later a shell landed just beyond a small rise. Pieces of wood were thrown a few yards into the air. 'There ya go, there's a bit of it now,' said the gunner laconically. 'An' it looks like it's a bit of foot-slogging for ya too, so good luck! Oh, an' tell 'em back there to send us a couple more joy-juice jars. We've bin dry fer weeks.'

* * *

Alec was delivered from the rapidly disintegrating duckboard track by motorcycle. At the aerodrome, for the first time in a couple of days, he could see his own boots. He sat on the edge of the landing strip and wrote a letter to Effie. All manner of planes were taking off and landing. An incongruous lone red flower fought the breeze. Alec was reminded of the loveliness of nature and the ingenuity of men, and wondered why the latter always seemed intent on crushing the former. At length he looked down at his finished page and tried to guess which words the censor would obliterate from the letter. He sighed. At least there wasn't an officer on earth who could obliterate the feelings he was beginning to have about Effie. He even wrote a letter to Bob just to say 'G'day', but doubted if it would ever reach him. The sinking orange sun illuminated his walking stick and soon darkness began to enfold the landing strip. Alec made for his designated hut, where a few of the boys were just heading off to a nearby estaminet.

Shell flashes sliced through the distant darkness like yellow and red knife blades. The occasional Very light added to the display. 'Strike me pink,' said Mick, one of the party. 'Ya wouldn't want to be out there ternight fer quids.'

'It was worse a couple of nights ago,' Alec said.

'Yeah,' said Paul, a Royal Flying Corps air mechanic. 'You wouldn't catch me up there!'

The others might well have chiacked him for this, except for the fact that Paul's left arm was in a sling and his fingers were a pulpy mass. He had received severe shrapnel wounds from a night bombing raid a few weeks before. The lads decided to save their disdain for the brass-hats who sat quaffing red wine in stately chateaux further towards the coast. One of the blokes who called himself Chas mumbled something about 'flamin' rosellas in the shatos drinkin' bookoo vin rooge', and strode on ahead to the estaminet, now in sight. He reached it — a building whose red brick and arched windows reminded Alec, even in the dark, of Cootamundra railway station — well ahead of the others, and was already in the company of two Frenchwomen and three beers by the time they arrived.

'Who are the tabbies, Chas?' asked Slim, a lance jack who had come over to the AFC from the Light Horse. 'They're givin' ya the glad eye all right.' Chas looked pleased. 'They shouted me three beers!'

As usual Alec ordered coffee.

'Are all you spooks wowsers, Griffo?' asked Mick.

'I'm not an artillery signaller, Mick, I've told you that already! I'm Flying Corps, through and through. And yes, I'm a wowser, and proud of it.'

The group sat at a table in the quiet cosiness of the estaminet, ate eggs and chips, drank, talked about home, and a few of their number sang a variant of an Australian Infantry song.

They changed the last line — which told of the Aussie Infantry earning six bob a day — to 'eight bob a day'. Emphasis on the 'eight' in 'eight bob a day' drew the ire of some nearby infantrymen (who now saw their six bob a day as a kick in the behind), and they got to their feet.

'No use droppin' yer bundle!' Chas called out. A cargo of beer was duly unloaded on the Infantry table, courtesy of the Flying Corps men.

Just before nine o'clock Chas stood up, more than a bit inky, and announced, 'I'd just like ter let ya all know that at five past nine Aussie beer can be purchased' — a mad rush of men leapt from their tables and made for the serving area — '... in all good pubs in Aussie. Your folks at home will tell ya all about it if yer write to 'em and ask nicely.' Chas grinned broadly. Every Digger in the estaminet turned and glared.

'Ya know why they call this place a jestaminnet? It's cos ya've got jestaminnet left to live!' shouted one of the infantrymen. Just as a wild brawl seemed imminent, Chas reached into his pocket and threw wads of French money at the men. 'Wait! No stoush — my shout.' The incident was soon forgotten, drowned in beer and laughter. Alec was happy. These boys were the closest thing to friends that he had on the Western Front, and he'd met them only a few hours before. And he would probably never see them again.

CHAPTER FOURTEEN
Bloody Passchendaele

It was raining again, without cease. Duckboards that had once connected the dugout to the guns had either sunk or simply floated away out of sight. The entire battery area, especially the dugout, was completely waterlogged. The mud had conquered everything. Men were sleeping on blankets so wet they were beginning to rot. About three feet of mud and water carpeted the bottom of the dugout. The dugout had very little shape or order to it, and Alec presumed it was probably just a hole made by a large artillery shell.

In the dugout the men stood thigh-deep in slush. For days, they shelled and were shelled. Shells blew men off their feet. When they regained consciousness, for some of them their feet were no longer there.

Alec saw a man get literally blown apart. He saw what happens when a shell detonates prematurely, before it has left the gun. He saw what high-explosive shrapnel can do to gunners out in the open: a nose-cap alone could decapitate a bloke. In front of his eyes a shell would kill two men, and another two would be untouched. Shells were not only impersonal, they were completely impartial as well.

With high-explosive shells, if you heard the whine of the incoming shell you could at least take steps to go to ground or dive into a hole, unless the task you were doing prevented you. Most of the time you couldn't hear them because you were so close to the line and the shells had such a flat trajectory. It was difficult to hear something whizzing through the air if it was not in the air long enough to be heard.

With high shrapnel, there was nothing you could do except hope. And in a bombardment, the ratio was usually one shrapnel shell in every five or six. The shells exploded in the air, above head height, and scattered shrapnel downwards. There really was nowhere to hide.

For days Alec laid out his white canvas strips on ground devoid of buildings or vegetation. Wherever there had been a church or a farmhouse he might find a few bricks scattered here and there, but even these would eventually disappear beneath the mud. Alec was one of the few living creatures above ground level and the German shells seemed intent on chastising him for being the only person stupid enough to remain there. Still, the job had to be done. Australian, British, Canadian and New Zealand infantrymen were relying on the artillery to engage the targets that impeded or threatened their progress. The shoots continued, until they blended into one. The strength of the battery dwindled. So did Alec's.

The nights were miserable, but by now Alec had grown accustomed to such misery. Nonetheless, every now and again he hoped for a Blighty hit or even just a blackout. Shells fell so close that the concussion would periodically extinguish the candle. Flares put up on parachutes to mark the area out at night were invariably followed by a quick bombardment. Either way, he could use the light of neither the candle nor the flares to write a Field Service Post Card to his mother. This was just as well, he reflected. Even had he been allowed to write whatever he liked, he would not have wanted her to know about what he had seen.

He had not been relieved in days. Occasionally he was shunted off to another battery nearby to do a shoot and then brought back to the one with the mass grave in its backyard. He had even been sent up to a forward infantry trench to conduct art-obs with the trench mortars. The shelling there was much less severe than he'd become accustomed to in the batteries, but the stench was worse. The area was thick with corpses, green with mildew. Even the trench itself had its dead. There was sorrow, but the men could not really afford grief. For these men, grief was a luxury that would have to be bought later. After a couple of shoots with the trench mortars Alec was almost glad to get back to his battery.

Shortly after his return, gas shells — mixed in with high explosive and shrapnel — soaked the area. Fortunately the strong winds dispersed the gas almost as soon as the men had reached for their ever-present canvas bags dangling from their necks. Wind played a terrific part in gas attacks. Sometimes there would be false alarms. At other times, the wind even blew the gas back onto the Germans themselves. The men were especially happy when that happened. The artillerymen did not stop what they were doing when gas hit. The gas mask was not incapacitating, and so within reason you just kept on with your job. Occasionally the gas would last a very long time. Sometimes it would get blown away, only to be blown back over the battery area again once the All Clear had been given.

The odour of phosgene was worse than the odour of the nearby shell holes that had become the latrines for the battery. The odour of corpses was worse than the smell of phosgene, and it seemed to invade even gas masks. There were no detergents to rid the area of this odour; just the black disinfectant of which nobody knew the name. The black disinfectant was always showered liberally on the areas of the battery positions where the dead had lain unburied for more than a couple of days, and this battery had received more than its fair share.

Clouds of diphenyl chlorasine gas — 'sneezing gas' or 'blue cross', which was meant to make the men tear off their gas masks in discomfort, only to be hit by the clouds of 'real gas' (mustard, chlorine or phosgene) — were certainly appearing more often now. Furphies that the Flanders campaign was winding down floated across the sea of mud around Passchendaele. Were they carried by the clouds of gas? It wouldn't be long now. It couldn't.

Despite the rumours, it seemed that the campaign was doing anything but winding down. The battery was being replenished with men more often than it was with shells, water or food. These 'fresh' men had to walk — run — through the mass grave behind the battery in order to get to the guns. Periodically Alec watched them arrive. Every now and again their eyes would meet. Alec was looking into the eyes of dead men, and *their* eyes knew it. One day Alec watched in horror as a group of reinforcements arrived at the same time that a five-point-nine landed. The force of the explosion buried three of them where they stood. The other two were thrown into the air and landed not as men but as piles of smoking, bloodied uniforms. The burial party took the afternoon off. There were no coffins, for the simple reason that there was no wood.

* * *

At stand-to Alec watched the day make its first movement towards dawn. Nothing stirred. The only living animals apart from the men of the battery were the vermin. In the estaminets, Alec had heard the infantry talk of large rats feeding off the corpses in the trenches and in no man's land. Out here in the artillery batteries, though, there were no rats — the shelling was too intense for them.

After stand-down the gunners went about cleaning their guns and arranging ammunition. Something was doing. A briefing by the battery commander confirmed this to Alec: another counter-battery shoot. A German battery had been menacing the Australian infantry for many days and causing tremendous casualties. Alec cleaned his wireless equipment as best he could, had an unpalatable breakfast of hard-tack rations washed down with a few mouthfuls of water that tasted like chlorine, and thought about the brass-hats back in their chateaux poring over red wine-stained battle maps that represented bloodstained tracts of land. He thought he felt bitter; perhaps it just saddened him. He knew that many a staff officer was killed by a shell or bomb in his headquarters, but at least back there his body could be found and given a decent burial.

The world erupted in a crash of a thousand guns. The shoot commenced not long afterwards, once an RE8 had flown over the battery from behind. The entire line was the arena for one great artillery duel. Alec did not envy the airmen. They established communications with him with difficulty as the blast of an incoming shell had blown the contact off his crystal. He prepared his canvas strips, orders were passed to the adjusting gun, the other guns prepared their ammunition accordingly. The usual messages arrived from the RE8 and the firing began. Above the bark of the lone 18-pounder, Alec heard the drone of an approaching machine. It was a red plane.

Alec's battery had been detected. Before long, a German adjusting gun was giving them some of their own back. But the shoot had to go on and they continued the laborious targeting procedure. They were slightly ahead of the Germans in the race to fire the first on-target salvo, but the Hun battery had a distinct advantage. It would soon have Alec's battery ranged and be bringing effective fire to bear, whereas in all probability the target of Alec's group was not that particular enemy battery. It would have free rein over them. Such are the fortunes of war.

A shell spiralled in and landed behind Alec's battery. Another landed in front. The Germans had them ranged. Minutes later a salvo landed. Then another, of high explosive and shrapnel. A lot of the gunners were hit. A man serving on the nearest gun to the dugout went to the aid of someone who had been hit, and was himself hit a few moments later. They died in each other's arms. Alec watched helplessly as another gunner picked pieces of shrapnel out of his screaming mate's back and carried him towards the dugout. More and more shells exploded. By the sheer weight of fire Alec felt certain there must have been more than one battery firing on them. Everywhere around him men were falling, dead or wounded. It was absolute pandemonium. The wounded gunner and the man who was carrying him were chopped down, only yards from the dugout. Neither moved again.

The battery could continue with its job only if Alec continued with his. He couldn't pause to try and help the fallen men. The incoming shells had slowed the battery's adjustment procedure, and only now were they able to fire a salvo. And then another. Men with minor shrapnel wounds continued to serve the guns. Their valour could not be described in words: Alec felt that all of them — to a man — deserved a DCM or even a Victoria Cross. But gunners were seldom awarded VCs.

Serve the guns! These words, in a gunner's heart, were more powerful than a divine order and it was almost as though the gunners knew, as Alec did, that their actions were saving many more lives in the Aussie infantry. Alec wanted to stay in the comparative safety of the dugout, but these gunners inspired him to go out in the open again. A high-explosive shrapnel shell burst nearby. Alec was hit. He was thrown to the sodden ground with the impact, and blood poured from his nose and ears and into his eyes. High explosive shells continued to burst all around him. Everything was noise, noise, noise. Somehow he realised that blood from your nose and ears should not get into your eyes. He put his hand to his forehead and found the source of the blood. Shrapnel had snuck beneath the sentry that his steel helmet was meant to be, and sliced his forehead. He tried to mop away the blood with his arm but encountered something very hard. He felt for the cut, to find that the shrapnel had torn away most of his forehead down to the bone. The hardness he was feeling was his own skull. A wave of shock and revulsion swept over him as he tried to get to his feet.

But he couldn't move. He just sat there, trying to wipe the blood away. A couple of men whose gun had been stonkered raced over to him. One of them gave him a drink of water, while the other — as casually as if he were attending to a minor gravel graze — pushed the two remaining pieces of Alec's forehead back into place and held them there. His mate got some shell dressing and dirty sticking plaster from the dugout and stuck flaps of flesh down. 'That'll see ya right, cob,' he said matter-of-factly.

Once the shoot had finished, Alec stumbled into the relative refuge of the dugout. It was filled with the sobs and cries of the wounded and dying. Casualties were not meant to be brought in here but there was nowhere else for them to go. A jar of rum was passed around the men, though some had no hands to hold it. Despite being teetotal, Alec guzzled the rum as if it was the most soothing, calming, delicious drink on earth. That day, it was.

* * *

The shelling continued for days. The horizon was ablaze. Gunners who had served at the Somme in 1916 swore that those battles — when it came to the sheer volume and relentlessness of the shelling — could not hold a candle to this one. Gunners who had survived the Somme were now being buried by walls of earth. They yelled and pleaded to be disinterred. By the time they were, most were dead. Yet other men were blown into pieces not much larger than the shell fragments themselves. There was no respite, even at night. The groans of wounded men seeped into the darkness until the darkness itself and death dissolved them. Occasionally shells would land so close at night that Alec and the others were temporarily blinded. A handful of men were so shell-shocked that they had lost their reason. They convulsed and sang meaningless words while the others tried to sleep, trying to forget. Alec dreamed of leave. He dreamed of Effie. He dreamed of Bob. He had never come closer to prayer than now.

The chance of anyone making their way out from a squadron to pick him up were minimal, and he resigned himself to staying here for some time yet in the mess they called Passchendaele. While many around him were losing their heads, he tried to keep his by carving more of his walking stick out of the propeller pieces. Coupled with the desire to catch up with Bob Lauchland, to meet Effie at long last and to see his family again, the carving was the only thing that kept him sane.

He moved to other batteries a few times but ended up back at the mass grave around the end of October. At least he thought that it was the same battery. Previously, dead meat tickets inscribed with the names of men had been slung over stakes. Now, the grave looked the same except that the handful of stakes had been blown clear. A more shell-smitten place on earth did not exist. None of the men were the same — Alec assumed they were all blow-ins. Am I the only one left alive?, he thought to himself. Somehow a letter from Effie had found its way out here. It was two months old. What was he doing? Had he heard from Bob? Was he enjoying being overseas? Did he like Europe? Why had he not answered all her letters? All he could think of was why you'd reply when you had nothing to say.

The battery was now literally drenched with gas of all types. It went on for days. Mustard gas — the baneful shell which the boys called 'yellow cross' — gave them a lot of casualties. Seeing what mustard gas did to people was not at all pleasant and Alec reeled at the sight of pallid-faced victims stretched out along the edge of the position, eyes bandaged and skin blistered. They were unable to walk or even stand upright. They were men who could not be helped. Each saw in his mind's eye his own family, his own town. Alec knew the feeling. Some of the men he saw stretched out there would probably never see again.

Phosgene? Well, he had grown used to that; the ever-present phosgene ensured that all the men kept their gas masks on for much of the time. But mustard gas? Was there no limit to the evil that the weapons people were creating? All the water near the battery had been contaminated by the chlorine from gas, and by bodies disinterred by shells. Without water resupply they'd all be dead men. Dead without wounds. It struck Alec as ironic, and he always made sure to greet the water resupply parties with a grin and a pat on the back. They were the salt of the earth.

CHAPTER FIFTEEN
'I am well'

'This war will end soon,' Alec's escort mused. There was scepticism in his optimism. The motorcycle whisked Alec out of the Passchendaele line in the first week of November, back to 'civilisation' at St Omer. Soldiers who had been up at the line and who were heading to rest billets in the rear eyed the reinforcements moving in the opposite direction. Pointing towards the line, they made gestures which spoke to the 'fresh' men of the unutterable. The civvies who lined the road were caricatures of Flemish misery. Only a Breughel painting could have done their dour faces justice. Indeed, blood was the only thing preventing the entire scene from being turned into a painting. There was even less left of Ypres than there had been before.

Alec tried to get news of his mate Bob, but nobody had heard any. He was billeted out to a farmhouse on the outskirts of a small village nearby. As he arrived, four women walked down the muddied and shell-torn street, clutching their skirts. A little boy kicked a ball. Otherwise nobody was to be seen. After knocking a few times on the door Alec could hear the sound of a recalcitrant bolt being drawn back. The door opened.

'Bonjour, Monsieur! Je m'appelle Claudette. Et vous?' Claudette had shoulder-length black hair — tousled by the sudden draught — ruby lips and black opal eyes. She was the very picture of loveliness. 'Bonshor, Mamzelle, I'm Alec Griffiths. Thank you for letting me lob here,' Alec replied. He picked up his kit and made to enter the musty farmhouse, but was halted by Claudette. Her sign language was as good as fluent English in saying, 'You can come in, but the lice stay outside.' He left as many items of kit and uniform outside that decency and dignity would allow, and she showed him to his room. She touched the bandages on his forehead, but he was still so infested with lice that the bandages were alive with them, right through to the wound, and he moved her hand away.

Sheets against skin! The feeling was too good to describe. He almost felt guilty, knowing there were still men out in the line, sleeping in mud. A wave of well-being swept over him as he opened the small pile of letters from Effie that had been waiting for him at the Depot. How he wanted to meet her! That she would continue to write, when almost all she ever received in return was 'I am well', was incredible. Such loyalty could only charm a bloke. He *knew* she was a very special girl, although he'd never met her. He yearned to hear the voice behind the words on the pages.

Alec got out of bed and went downstairs, the smell of coffee proving a greater lure than the feel of the bed sheets. He was hoping that Claudette could tell him something about a woman who would continue to write to a man she hadn't met. But Claudette was more concerned with making the coffee, and besides, she didn't speak a word of English.

After a couple of days a motorcycle and sidecar came to collect him and he was taken back to St Omer. Everyone there seemed dead tired. The Passchendaele campaign had taken its toll on the living as well. So much had happened so quickly at Passchendaele: history wasn't meant to happen that fast. In the space of a few weeks it had become part of the gunners' country, part of Alec's country. It belonged to them, as much as Australia itself did.

Around the middle of November 1917 he was posted to No. 2 Squadron AFC (née No. 68 Squadron RFC) at Warloy, near

Baizieux. It was a fighter squadron without wireless, so the idea was that he'd be used in the Somme sector for art-obs with Tommy batteries, while being 'administered' by an Australian squadron. Wireless operators were still terribly scarce, even with the Ypres offensive now finished. Most of them had been killed. And the brass-hats couldn't just pluck them off the shelf.

Warloy was a bitterly cold place. Fortunately Alec received a few parcels from Australia while he was here. All of them contained socks. These were very much appreciated, but most of them weren't all too comfortable. It wasn't hard to imagine that there were a lot of people back home knitting socks who weren't too good at the idea. The socks were very rough around the heels and gave Alec blisters, but he found that warm feet with blisters were infinitely preferable to frozen feet without. He was happy to receive them. Although the socks helped warm the feet, the people in Australia had yet to send a parcel containing something to stop his hair freezing into icicles, or to stop his boots freezing to the floor during the night as if glued.

The aerodrome at Warloy was an interesting place. In addition to seeing the squadron's DH5s, Alec caught glimpses of the famed Sopwith Pups. The Pups went out on patrol frequently, and just as frequently these little blokes would return with one of their number missing, or quite badly shot up.

There was a sergeant-major at Warloy who, almost every day, took his washing down into the village. There was also a little estaminet down in the village, run by a couple of very good-looking girls. The sergeant-major seemed intent on perpetuating the widely held belief among many of the Australians that AIF stood not only for Australian Imperial Forces, but also for Admired In France. Alec always reckoned that the estaminet was his direction and target, not the laundrette. Either this, or he washed his uniforms every day. But he was, after all, a sergeant-major, and no one was game to challenge him. Not even the officers.

Conditions on the Somme were bitter. The cold almost defied description; any water on the ground froze at night. When snow melted it added to the mud, turning much of the battlefield into slush. This battlefield became the scene of the first massed tank attack in history: the Battle of Cambrai. Besides the men from the 2nd Squadron AFC and a handful of siege artillerymen, Alec was one of the few Australians to serve in this battle. For days beforehand, the noise of grinding tanks could be heard constantly. The lumbering monsters were about the strangest things Alec ever saw in the war. He had seen these unwieldy 'fighting tanks' with their peculiar 'chains' on each side back in the Ypres sector in early October, and how they managed to do the jobs assigned to them was a mystery to him.

To get into position the tanks had to go through very soft ground and across all manner of obstacles. They seemed literally to be walking across the landscape, making a frightful noise as they went. Now, in the whole sector there were dozens upon dozens of them, and they pulverised ground that had hitherto seemed beyond further punishment.

There was no preliminary bombardment for the Battle of Cambrai, but after the stunt was under way there was to be artillery observation. The Tommy observation planes were used to correct artillery fire whenever possible and to direct fire onto 'targets of opportunity'. Few enemy shells actually landed near Alec's battery, whose targets by and large were troop formations. In the ensuing days, things changed, the battery being employed in firing on active German batteries. Increasingly they fired back. The German observation machines became very active in registering the Allied batteries, and casualties mounted to the point where they had to withdraw.

* * *

At the end of November Alec moved again to No. 3 Squadron AFC (the old 69th), this time at Bailleul. Bailleul! Such a sweet-sounding name. It had once been beautiful, but now it would not be long until it was little more than a heap of ruins. Bailleul was just another ravaged village in a sea of ruined French towns and villages, whose womenfolk had been compensated by their government with a money order for a few hundred francs for every *poilu* family member killed in action. A few hundred francs for a son. A few hundred francs for a brother.

Bailleul, too, was just another home to another squadron that had to feed Alec Griffiths. They were providing support for I (ANZAC) Corps, but nonetheless Alec was once again to spend more time with Tommy and Canadian batteries than he would with Australian ones. While he was at Bailleul, news of the Bolshevik Revolution in Russia filtered down to the men of the AFC. Most of them became pretty concerned as to what effect this would have on them. Would it release a lot more Hun soldiers to fight on the Western Front? It was a very real prospect, and their gravest fear.

But for Alec, it was as nothing compared with the news he now received. Bob Lauchland was dead.

Apparently Bob had been seriously wounded by shrapnel back up in the Ypres sector while laying out the white canvas strips during a shoot. It was the fate of most Flying Corps wireless operators. He had been hospitalised but had later died of wounds.

Alec's best mate had been taken from him. Just like that. The tears came for days after that. The anguish never really stopped.

Alec desperately wanted to find Bob's grave, if indeed he had one, so that he could say the goodbye he'd never had the chance to say. But he was just one of thousands of blokes whose mates had been killed. No one could tell him where he could find Bob. Alec vowed that one day he would find his best mate's grave, and say farewell. One day.

* * *

In December 1917 the question of conscription came up again in Australia. There was quite a bit of talk about it around the traps on the Western Front — the AFC men had to vote, just like the people in Australia. But Alec felt that the people didn't really have anything to do with it; it was the politicians who wanted to keep the war going, who continued to send boys off to be killed. The soldiers were only fighting because it was their duty. Alec had seen examples of mateship that had no equal, and unsurpassed acts of courage.

He had watched as men laid down their lives for the good of the many, disregarding the life of the one. He had watched as Diggers and Enzeds tried to help their mates, knowing full well that it would mean their own death. At the third battle of Ypres the Australians had given a superlative account of themselves and knew they had done their fledgling nation proud. But this, Alec felt, did not justify helping the slaughter to continue. He voted No.

One day, late in December 1917, Alec loaded his equipment into a Crossley tender and was soon on his way to another aerodrome. As they drove away, he fancied he saw his brother Lock loading some wireless equipment into a motorcycle's sidecar. It couldn't be. Lock was in the merchant navy. How could he possibly be here, on the Western Front? Instinct made Alec call out to him: 'Hey, brother!' The man looked up and waved, but it was not in recognition. It was the wave that people make in a case of mistaken identity, and they just wish to be courteous. Of course it couldn't be Lock. Alec folded his arms, feeling very silly. Perhaps in his yearning for a familiar face he was beginning to see things.

There were no real celebrations for Christmas. The boys didn't have much to celebrate with anyhow. Alec spent Christmas Eve in the dugout of a Tommy battery, huddled over a small brazier, finishing off carving the handle of his walking stick. The coke fumes were almost suffocating but it was either put up with them or die of cold. Dozens of them huddled in this labyrinthine dugout, barely able to breathe.

Despite the brazier, it was almost midday before any feeling came back into Alec's feet. Frostbite had already hit a couple of the gunners. They refused to tell their superiors about it, because having frostbite in the British Army was a punishable offence. So was sporting the telltale black horror of trench feet. Alec reckoned that the real punishable offence was sending men into conditions like this in the first place. It was also a punishable offence in the British Army to cut down the long infantry greatcoats in order to make progress through the knee-deep mud a little bit easier. Despite accounts of men having tripped on their own coats and come a gutser into a frozen shell hole and perished, the British brass-hats refused to change the regulation. Alec was glad to be an Australian.

Out here, in the fields of France among the snowdrifts, it was almost beautiful — even the fragments of ice that floated in chlorine-contaminated water at the bottom of the dugout. After Passchendaele, everything was a joy. The smell of shirts filthy with sweat, the glow of the brazier, the weary limbs, life itself. Life especially.

There were still the hardships. It was a winter of frequent and heavy snowstorms. The temperature seldom climbed above zero. Feet sank into the ground and froze solid. The acrid, choking fumes of exploding shells never completely dissipated. Alec and the other men were constantly wet through and rotting in the crotch and feet. Mornings found them with their mouths and noses iced up, their breath having condensed and frozen during their few hours of sleep. The cold did provide some 'comfort', however. It ensured that the vermin obtained less of a foothold. Alec still had to run a candle down the seams of his uniform to get rid of them periodically, but they were not as thick as they had been.

Though this wasn't Passchendaele, there were still the ever-present reminders of death. Whenever the snow melted, the hands of the dead began to show. In some macabre way the scene reminded Alec of tree stumps sticking up out of a field of wildflowers. He knew that if he survived the war he would never be able to look at the carved hand that formed the grip of his walking stick without thinking of this scene. But for the moment, Bob's death weighed heavily. That, and Alec's six months of salt meat and little else, the continual shortage of clean water, and a series of shrapnel wounds, were exacting their toll. Alec was no longer 'well'.

The ration, water and ammunition parties seldom came. They often became bogged or, even worse, lost. Sometimes the water resupply didn't arrive for days. In such cases the men had to drink water from the shell holes, the surfaces of which had frozen over. There was always the very real risk of contamination, but they reckoned that it was too cold for animal and human corpses to rot and so they took their chances. There were a few men who could not bring themselves to drink of the same shell-hole water in which they had seen their mates die. They sucked the moisture out of sandbags or, if time permitted, quarried ice from the locale and melted it in sandbags over the brazier. To perish of thirst in such a wet place would have seemed so senseless. At least Alec was being taken out of the line quite frequently now. More than the respite from the miserable conditions, this meant that he could correspond more frequently with Effie Melville.

CHAPTER SIXTEEN
Blighty

Take me back to dear old Blighty
Blighty is the place for me.

Soldiers' song

A few weeks after Alec turned eighteen years of age in the wasteland of frozen mud that was the Somme, a duckboard harrier arrived with a message. He was a tall, muscular man but the Somme winter had not been kind to him and the umber skin on his face and hands looked like Flanders mud. The chewed-down nails on his fingers spoke of one of the most nerve-racking jobs a bloke could ever do: runner. He spoke as rapidly as drumfire, a little breathlessly, looking straight into the eyes of the battery commander and every now and then turning to Alec, as though he were somehow involved in some fiendish plot.

So it was that, after six months on active service and while still serving as a wireless operator in an artillery battery at the Somme, Alec was told he was going back to England. He had no idea why, and neither did anybody else. He felt he should have been excited, but emotions were numb.

On 21 January 1918 Second Class Air Mechanic Alec Griffiths

was officially transferred to the Home Establishment. At last he was leaving the troglodytic realm, an old man. Unlike the infantrymen, Alec had never really experienced machine-gun fire. There had been so much noise of everything else, you didn't really ever hear just machine-gun fire; what he had endured was six months of shelling, shelling that had driven many men mad. He had endured misery and absolute loneliness. He had endured the Somme. And he had survived Passchendaele. He was tired.

Eventually Alec learned why he had been taken permanently out of the line. As one of the few wireless operators on the Western Front who had not been killed, crippled or sent insane, he had been selected to return to Australia to help establish a school for wireless operators. At the rate they were being consumed by the engine that was the Great European War, the supply of fuel was running out faster than it could be supplied and a new source, it was thought, would have to be found within six to nine months. The school was to be formed by the Australian Flying Corps. But first Alec had to undergo further training in England and also to remain on stand-by there for the time being in case the wireless operator casualty rate went off the scale again, as it had in the Third Battle of Ypres.

He ended up staying in France a couple of weeks longer, until 6 February 1918. He was then transferred from No. 2 Squadron AFC to Army Headquarters in England, via a great long shed, 100 yards long, where he was given a final delousing. His uniforms and equipment were burned.

In London, Alec was blissfully reminded that there was more to the world than dugouts, shrapnel, mud, bloodstained uniforms and corpses. There were fog-fringed sunsets, untainted by the acrid fumes of shell smoke. There was real food. There were girls. There was dancing. And there was laughter. And the best thing? The Underground. Here a man could exist under the earth, without the looming prospect that it could bury him alive. The Western Front suddenly seemed like a bizarre, evil work of fiction. After a couple of weeks in London, learning how to be a gentleman again, he was sent to the (now) Royal Air Force No. 1 Wireless School at

Farnborough. Here he studied the latest developments in continuous wave transmission and wireless telephony, both of which were in their infancy.

At the end of May he was taken on strength at the No. 7 Training Squadron, at the AFC Depot at Leighterton, where he was promoted to the dizzy heights of first class air mechanic. At last he was among the dinkums again.

That was all very well but Alec wanted to get to Scotland to meet Effie at long last and to comfort the family in their grieving over the death of Bob Lauchland. He wanted to go for Bob's sake and to tell the family what little he knew of Bob's last days. After pleading with the appropriate brass-hats for several months, Alec finally wangled some leave and was granted a pass.

He arrived in Bo'ness, Scotland, on a Friday night in October. After leaving the train he wandered the dark streets, looking for the Melville home. At length he walked by a high building, where something made him look up. There, leaning out over a flower box and cleaning the windows, was the prettiest, most captivating girl he had ever seen.

Was she beautiful? Or was she lovely? Was this the lass who had been writing to him? Was this the one for whom his heart had been searching? He returned her innocent wave, and before Alec knew it she was standing beside him, this girl who seemed to be all his dreams rolled up into one. At last he was beside this Effie whom he had waited so long to see.

He managed a stammer. 'I'm ... Alec.'

'Ah know who y'are, my sweet Alec. Ah knew you'd come,' she smiled. As she took him inside she confided in a delicious Scottish accent, 'When ah saw you doon below in the street, how ah hoped this handsome young Aussie in mil'tary uniform would turn oot to be mah Alec.'

As a result of those words it was a blushing young Digger who was introduced to her mother and father, her brothers Andrew and Bill, and sisters Alice and Nan. Nan was a mischievous imp, who immediately began teasing big sister and her Australian beau.

Alec spent the weekend at the Melville house, Effie and he getting to know each other better. After the correspondence between them during Alec's time in England and on the Western Front, it was more like getting reacquainted with an old friend than meeting someone for the first time. Alec told Effie a little of the times he had been wounded, but spared her the details. It was enough that she kissed him lightly on the forehead, which had now healed. They reminisced about a wonderful man — a wiry young Queenslander called Bob Lauchland. They laughed. They cried. The weekend concluded, almost as soon as it had begun, with a Sunday 'high tea'. Also present at this gathering were Granny Melville from Polmont and Uncle Tom, a barrister and lay preacher who resided nearby. Uncle Tom, Alec soon learned, was extremely straitlaced. He was also a self-appointed family selection board. Anyone entering the family fold had first to overcome his disdain and then earn his approval. Alec found himself getting the once-over. Fortunately, Uncle Tom was distracted by little Nan who, sitting in the corner with her dolls and Alec's slouch hat, began to giggle uncontrollably.

'Aye,' she chortled, 'it's such a funny lewking hoot.'

'Whisht, lassie,' Uncle Tom admonished. 'Dinna carry on like that on ter Lord's day.'

Their time together, Effie and Alec's, had been as precious as it was limited. The things he would have liked to say, but didn't for worrying about how much his shyness and inexperience would hamper him, Alec had no opportunity to try out. Each time the breakaway words rose, they got held up at a cattle-grid in his throat. As it happened, almost every minute he spent with her they were surrounded by the warm, welcoming Melville family. They talked some more about Bob, whom all of them loved. Alec could not even mention Bob's name without bursting into tears. At least here with this wonderful family, away from the inestimable suffering and liquefied clay of the Western Front, away from a land where even the soil bled, a soldier could cry.

At Polmont station, there was little time to say goodbye. Many eyes were on the slouch-hatted Australian as he boarded the train, but he only had eyes for one. As the train pulled out, Alec leaned out of the rickety window and watched as Effie seemed to grow smaller on the platform. He plucked up enough courage to yell out, 'Will you wait for me?' He couldn't hear what she said, if she said anything at all. But he knew the answer by the way she looked at him and waved, her damp white handkerchief fluttering in the side draught created by the train.

A week later, Alec was making his way from Halefield Camp Wendover to Plymouth. On 19 October 1918 Alec was put on board the troopship *Sardinia*, Destination Known. With him, and some 30 other men who had been chosen to help establish the Flying Corps wireless school in Australia, were hundreds of sick and wounded soldiers.

PART III

HOME!

CHAPTER SEVENTEEN
The Scent of Eucalyptus

For what seemed like a week, the troopship lay in port. On two occasions a Royal Navy band played them a send-off with the melancholy strains of 'Good-bye-ee', but the *Sardinia* didn't actually sail. The captain had decided to wait for a foggy night in order to sneak out of Plymouth and avoid German submarines lurking in the area. Conditions aboard the ship were less than hygienic, with no ventilation to speak of. Finally they got away.

The *Sardinia* had been at sea for only a fortnight when the men heard that the Armistice had been signed. There was no rejoicing, however, as the ship had a severe epidemic on board and many victims were being put over the stern each night, secretly buried at sea. In addition, dozens of men were dying from pneumonia, brought on by having been gassed on the Western Front. Furphies were rife among the Aussies that the epidemic was black plague (though this could well have been Spanish influenza) spread by the rats and through faulty ventilation in the cargo holds. This would have been no problem were it not for the fact that it was in the cargo holds that the returning Diggers — these men who had fought so valiantly for their country — were being accommodated. There was no jollification on the ship whatsoever, despite the news that the war to end all wars had, itself, ended. Some of the sick men were in such misery that they tried to hurl themselves overboard, and had to be restrained.

The Australians were enduring rough weather out in the middle of nowhere; men dying, the crew not knowing how many were dying, just sewing them up in weighted canvas bags and throwing them over the side. The officers thought there was no one watching. They were wrong. Alec could only look on, helplessly, as the numbers in his cargo hold dwindled, as dozens of corpses were thrown into the sea.

The drinking water in the tank was red with Condy's crystals. It was an admission if there ever was one that there had been an outbreak of serious illness on board. Alec's 'living area' teemed with vermin. The entire ship was riddled with them. The lifebelts were stored in racks above the tables and were so thick with vermin that the lice would drop in their dozens into the Diggers' food while they were eating. The vermin had been unbelievable in Flanders; after a time Alec had given up trying to get rid of them. Even in dugouts that had been vacated for a while, they'd still be there. They had been so thick that they'd lived off each other. The soldiers on the *Sardinia* had thought they'd left the lice behind forever. And yet here they were still, almost as if following the men.

Something else would soon be following them. The time grew near for the big sighting. Every night, sleepless eyes and homesick hearts roamed the skies for the first glimpse of the Southern Cross. The beacon that pointed to home; the only bright spot on the entire voyage home. The search went on for hours into the night, as there was no telling exactly when the sparkling white opals would appear. The men didn't have the means to predict it.

Rather than band together on deck and cheer in groups, when the Cross finally appeared most of the soldiers found their own little corner of the ship and looked up at that most glorious of sights. Alec remembered gazing at its brilliant light in 1916, and he thought of all that had come to pass since then. He wept quietly, but no one saw.

The *Sardinia* arrived in Albany on Christmas Eve 1918 and anchored in King George Sound. The men weren't permitted ashore on account of the disease. General William Birdwood had given all the men a 'Merry Christmas' message, yet they spent Christmas Day confined to the squalor of the troopship. The next few days were spent taking on fresh water, coal and supplies. The breeze brought with it the scent of eucalyptus. It was wondrous. The men wanted to reach out to the peppermint gums and touch them; to walk on the land of their youth once more.

Their *youth*? By now this ship — the home of a thousand invalids — was a ship of men whose youth, despite their average age of 23 or so, had been lost forever. They spent New Year's Eve at sea. There was little to celebrate. On New Year's Day the pre-dawn light was reflected in the ocean as Alec gazed landwards. Then the upturned bowl of sky slowly filled with a pinkish-blue liquid, extinguishing the stars. On that day Alec even forgot that it was his nineteenth birthday.

The first day of 1919 saw the *Sardinia* arrive at Port Phillip Bay, only for the men to be quarantined once again. Any happiness the men had felt on moving through the Heads turned to rage. Fortunately the Red Cross, the soldiers' angels, relieved the situation a little by bringing out comforts to the returned men.

After a couple of days within sight and smell of their homeland the men were informed they were finally to be allowed ashore. A lot of the troops, including Alec, were bound for their home port, Sydney or Brisbane, aboard the *Sardinia*. But they decided that once they got ashore here in Melbourne they wouldn't go back to the ship because it was riddled with vermin and disease. On the day the *Sardinia* was to be tied up at Port Melbourne, the men went around the entire ship and threw every single lifebelt, kapok-filled life jacket, blanket and hammock overboard. Their reasoning was simple: this way the returned soldiers could not be taken any further on the ship. Some of the officers started shouting 'Mutiny!'

but the men informed them that, because they weren't the ship's crew, there was Buckley's chance of making the charge stick. There was nothing the officers could do except take the men ashore.

They were greeted by a team of private cars with volunteer civilian drivers, as the brass-hats had refused to allow military vehicles and personnel to pick them up. They were taken to Victoria Barracks in St Kilda Road, where they were given a much needed delousing, a hot bath and a complete change of clothing including uniform and civvies. After attending a 'welcome home' dinner — also organised with the assistance of civvy volunteers, since the military heads had refused to do anything — Alec was sent on disembarkation leave for a couple of days, then ushered into a sleeper berth on a train bound for Sydney.

He couldn't say it had been enjoyable coming home. It hadn't been. The fact that he was getting home was the main thing. Out of the train window Alec watched as the grey-blue of the Australian bush slipped past in majestic silence, to be devoured by the warm bronze twilight performance that only Australia knows how to put on. He smiled. He smiled for a long time. The lights of the sleeper berth cast their diffuse glow on the passing box-ironbark forests and candlebarks of northern Victoria before he stopped smiling.

He had already played the arrival scene over in his mind. Thousands would be there to welcome them. On his arrival in Sydney, Alec and the other passengers enthusiastically flung open the carriage doors, like villagers throwing open their window-shutters to greet a passing street parade.

There was no one there. Where were the parades, the garlands of flowers, the young girls carrying the seeds of kisses to be planted on soldiers' cheeks, the old men with tears in their eyes? None were to be found. Perhaps it was just too early, perhaps these men were the first Diggers to return after the Armistice. That must be it, Alec thought. And in fact there was a considerable delay in getting the rest of the 1st AIF home. Most of them were billeted in France for the winter and wouldn't get home until the Australian autumn. Their discontent reached the press in Australia, and rightfully so.

Before Alec left England he was supposed to have signed on for another five years, in order that he could help get the Flying Corps wireless school up and running. However, the signing on had somehow been omitted from his schedule of things to do. Now that he was back in Australia, he was naturally more intent on preparing himself for his future life than giving five more years to the Army. He was all for getting out, and the Army was all for keeping him there. 'You were meant to sign on for five years. You can't get a discharge,' they told him. 'Oh yes I can,' Alec replied. 'You've got no undertaking of mine beyond the expiration of the war.' In fact they did. At enlistment he had, without reading it fully, signed the standard declaration to serve until the end of the war, and 'a further period of four months thereafter unless sooner lawfully discharged, dismissed, or removed therefrom ...'. Eventually he was granted his discharge — four months later, in April 1919.

* * *

The newly designated Mr Alec Griffiths was issued with 'civilian suit and cap', and donned civvies for the first time in two years and 219 days. Of this period, according to his discharge certificate, two years and 32 days had been spent serving overseas in the Australian Imperial Expeditionary Forces. They had been the longest days of his life. As he had been at war during the time he should have been doing his apprenticeship, the Australian government gave him vocational training. He was placed with an electrical firm called Coupland & Waddell, in Day Street, and the award wage he was paid was shared between the firm and the government on a sliding scale which proved satisfactory to Alec. Other Diggers were not so lucky. Many, under the Soldier Settlement Scheme, were given parcels of land out in the backblocks. For the bushmen this was a blessing. But for the townies with no experience of farming, a parcel of land back of Bourke was like a life sentence.

Alec had been so looking forward to seeing his family again. He learned that Fred and Lock had survived. Fred was serving as wireless operator on the *Makambo*, plying the Pacific Ocean between Australia and the New Hebrides. Lock was in England, but no one had bothered to write to Alec and tell him this when he was still there. Eliza Jane cried with joy when she first saw Alec; she was one of the few mothers in Australia whose three sons had gone off to war and survived. Alec's sisters wanted to know what the war had been like. He didn't reply, feeling that an eyewitness account would only upset and confuse them. The look on his face was the same that crossed thousands of other men's faces every time a kid asked, 'What's war like?'. It was a look that, like war itself, couldn't be truly described unless one had seen it.

One of Alec's first jobs involved the ships that transported bananas from Fiji. These ships carried absolutely nothing else but bananas; after their arrival vendors would run along the streets of Sydney shouting 'Fiji bananas! Fiji bananas! A yard long and a foot thick! Get yer Fiji bananas!' And they weren't far off it, either.

Coupland & Waddell had the contract to repair the electrical gear on the ships. One particular bloke Alec worked with, Len, always got the job of repairing some of the electrical gear actually on board the ship (it couldn't be removed for repair like most of the other gear) because he was used to it and, therefore he argued, the best at it. He always went down into the ship with plenty of room in his bag for bananas. He seldom even worried about his tools, and just brought back a bag of bananas off the ship with him. Len would always come up to the office just before knock-off time, and set the bag down in front of his locker. For Len, 'time to knock-off' meant 'time to knock off some Fiji bananas'. The lads would always see the bag was full of bananas, and they reckoned they would have to do something about that.

One day the boys arranged that they would keep an eye on Len while a couple of the men pulled the bananas out of his bag just before knock-off time, put a couple of clouts into the floor through the bag, and put the bananas back in. Len, who was cutting it fine for catching his train home, came into the office in a tearing hurry and grabbed his bag on the run. The bottom came out of his bag. Bananas flew in all directions, and Len looked as though his mother had just died. The boys apologised to him because they had simply thought that he would have been unable to pick up his bag, and that would be it. Anyhow, the boys took up a collection to buy Len a new bag. He accepted, on the proviso that they buy him a much bigger bag.

Events like the Fiji banana episode were times to be cherished in Alec's post-war days. Though the memories of Flanders would never fade, at least they could be hidden every now and again behind the painted veil of fun times. Alec enjoyed his new job. The job was not at all well paid, but he was among mates. Mates that he had not had the opportunity to have in the war. That's what counted. And he could work happily, free of the fear of being shelled. He didn't get to save very much of his pay, but he reckoned not too many returned Diggers did. They had to take what came.

* * *

Life was not meant to be easy, nor was it, back in Australia. Being a returned serviceman made you a little special, but you couldn't live off being a returned man. Especially if you were a man with pieces missing. There were no handouts to be had either. And being an invalid might as well have been a crime, considering the way the government treated you. In 1919 the average weekly earnings for civilian workers were between three and four pounds a week. But if you were unfortunate enough to have become a double amputee in the service of your country, the war pension gave you between two and three pounds per week. If you were fortunate enough to have lost only one eye, one arm and one leg, your country paid you exactly two pounds two shillings per week. And if you had lost only one leg, your war pension was a trifle more than a third of the average weekly earnings. Alec was immeasurably grateful for his narrow escape from death at Passchendaele, for his health, and most of all for his job. What the pension would have been if Australia had *lost* the war didn't bear thinking about.

Lock returned home in the winter of 1919. The day they met him you could have knocked Alec over with a feather. 'Strike me pink,' he exclaimed. After that, he was speechless for minutes. In place of the uniform of the merchant navy, Lock was sporting the jaunty-angled slouch hat and the familiar uniform of the Australian Flying Corps. First Class Air Mechanic Alec Griffiths had come face to face with Second Class Air Mechanic Harold Griffiths.

'Give me a hug, Lock,' Alec ordered. 'Why?' said Lock, grinning cheekily. 'Cos I outrank you, Griffiths!' They embraced, and adjourned to the nearest pub verandah to yarn about the Flying Corps. Despite Lock's elation at tasting his first Aussie beer in years, Alec asked for a coffee. The publican looked at him quizzically. 'Will a cuppa tea do, mate?'

Lock had transferred from the merchant navy to the Australian Flying Corps in 1916 and had seen service in Mesopotamia as a wireless operator. He had later been sent to the Western Front in France where he spent 1917 and 1918. And yes, he had been at Bailleul in late 1917. It must have been Lock that Alec waved to; but it was a triviality now. The two brothers may well have served at the same artillery battery at different times, or maybe even in adjacent batteries at the same time. Neither would ever know and perhaps that was a good thing.

Lock, it eventuated, had been involved in some of the big stunts of 1918. He had been in France during the signing of the Armistice, before being transferred back to England in early 1919 after spending another winter in rest billets in France. Lock didn't say much about what he had seen and experienced amid the horrors of the Western Front. He simply looked across the head of his third beer at Alec with a glance that said, 'I know that you know, little brother.'

That same year, Ross and Keith Smith arrived in Australia after their record-breaking flight from London in a Vickers-Vimy bomber. They took long enough on their way out to Australia for the newspapers to report their progress. They landed in Darwin to a hero's welcome. It was a real red letter day. Alec was proud of his Australian Flying Corps brethren; that a machine of war could at last be used for some greater purpose was indeed a great symbol of hope. Later in the year, Alec was most interested to read in the newspaper that the first transcontinental flight across Australia — from Point Cook to Darwin — had been a success. It took the better part of a month. Memories of flying over the Western Front flooded back to him as he read the name of one of the two pilots: Captain H.N. Wrigley.

The year 1919 was also when Alec bought his first motorcar — or at least the chassis of one. It was a Berliet, built in 1914. The chassis was sitting in a paddock up near Parramatta and was ridden with rust. Alec bought it for £30, taking it back to Sydney on the blue metal and dirt road on a hired four-wheeled, flat-topped lorry drawn by two horses. To earn some money he overhauled it in the ensuing months and sold it later for £60 'as is'. For returned men to make a quid or two it was pretty tough, but Alec reckoned that fixing up motorcars was as good a way as any. So he bought a few more and did the same thing. One that he purchased was a 1914 Unic, a vertical twin-cylinder job. He paid 30 quid for it and sold it for 50 after getting it running.

Alec bought these cars as derelicts. They had been abandoned to the elements because their owners couldn't obtain petrol during the war. By the time the war was over, there were so many derelicts littering the Australian bush and the suburbs that horses outnumbered working cars by at least 200 to one. The railway stations, in particular, were always surrounded by horse-cabs, like seagulls waiting for leftover food scraps at the beach. The driver sat up top in the rain while the passengers sat inside. Almost every returned soldier who hadn't started a farm in the outback or got a job with the railways or the tramways was driving these horse-cabs. Or so it seemed.

After becoming a journeyman electrician, Alec soon found that he no longer had time to buy and sell motorcars. Increasingly he was on call to deal with electrical breakdowns, something he had volunteered to do in order to earn extra money. He had one goal in mind: to save enough money to bring Effie Melville out to Australia.

* * *

Two-and-a-half years after having met her, Alec wrote and invited Effie to join him. They had been corresponding regularly during their time apart and had not only grown close but had come to know each other well. Well enough, Alec felt, for him to pop the question. He had never once thought of going out with girls now he was back in Australia. All he had been concerned with was to earn enough money to buy a house and bring Effie out. That was the way things were. A bloke would always make sure he was financially secure before he asked a girl to marry him.

There were no air mail deliveries then; the mail went by ship on a six- or seven-week journey. Tension and uncertainty built up exponentially in Alec as the weeks went by. He had a cousin about his own age, Charlie, who had also experienced the same waiting. Charlie, who had served in the Australian infantry on the Somme and also in the Ypres sector, had also fallen in love with a girl from the British Isles and arranged to bring her out. On the voyage she fell in love with a chap she met on the ship. The first Charlie got wind of this was when she arrived. He had shouted her the fare out to Sydney, too. He didn't ask for it back, he didn't see the point. But he did see the point in going down to the pub and getting rotten drunk. None of this augured well for Alec. Nonetheless, thirteen weeks after he'd written he received Effie's reply. It had been, Alec reckoned, the longest period of time in history that a bloke had had to wait for a reply to a marriage proposal. His hands shook as he opened the letter. It said, simply, 'Yes!'

Alec made arrangements for her passage out to Sydney on the SS *Ceramic*. The fare was £90, for a bunk in a four-berth cabin in steerage. Effie arrived months later. To meet her at the wharf the Griffiths family hired a motor taxi. Alec was anxious to get Effie home but his mother, ever conscious of her civic duty, almost threw a spanner in the works when a traffic accident occurred in front of the taxi. A policeman approached her, seeking the required witness.

'What did you see, please m'am?'

Eliza Jane, sitting in the front next to the driver, began, 'I saw ...'

In the blink of an eye Alec realised what would happen. He leaned forward and thundered to his mother, 'You saw *nothing*!'

Alec and Effie were married that very day, the day she first set foot on Australian soil. It was 5 November 1921 — Guy Fawkes

Day. Clearly it had been an enormous challenge for Effie to come alone to a country where she knew no one except Alec. Even then, Alec was only a man she had seen for a brief weekend, in the familiar surrounds of her family and their home. Alec's little schoolteacher belle from far-off Bo'ness, Scotland, must indeed have been a woman of great courage to brave, under these circumstances, a country which her compatriots regarded as being one of 'kangaroos and uncivilised blackfellows, mostly'.

The wedding, prearranged by Alec's family, was a splendid little affair. It was held at the Glebe Presbyterian Church, and Effie carried November lilies and wore evocative perfume. Alec's groomsmen were his brothers John and Lock.

For their honeymoon, Alec and Effie travelled by train to Katoomba. In the 1920s that was the thing to do. Alec would perhaps have liked a more exotic and less frequented place, but he had little money left and in any case wanted to show Effie the unparalleled beauty of the Australian bush and its towering eucalypts. The time they spent together in the Blue Mountains, the solitude of long walks in the bush, brought them closer together and they became the best of friends as well as lovers. They both felt that Bob was watching over them; that he knew that Alec and Effie were meant to be together.

CHAPTER EIGHTEEN

Building a Life

The day is short and the work is long.

Proverb

Despite having given up repairing cars, early in 1922 Alec started buying motorbikes to do up and sell in order to make an extra few bob. His favourite was a particular BSA with sidecar. He liked it so much that he kept it, even though after he'd rescued it from a rusty grave and repaired it to its former glory it was eminently saleable. It became the first motor vehicle he owned that he actually got around on.

The BSA didn't have a clutch or a gearbox. The drive train consisted of a V-pulley on the crankshaft of the oil-smeared engine and a larger V-pulley on the back wheel, with a rubber belt in between. That was it. The bike wasn't real flash in wet weather, as the belt would slip. One day Alec got caught in a storm out on the Parramatta Road in Homebush, and the only way he could get home was to wrap sticking tape around the drivebelt to stop it from slipping. The fact that Parramatta Road was little more than a dirt track turned to mud didn't help matters. Memories of the corduroy road out of Ypres flooded into Alec's mind. He looked around for shell holes, found none, and smiled to himself.

But the BSA was quick. Apart from slamming on the brakes, the only way to slow it down was to stop the engine firing by means of a lever on the handlebars that lifted the exhaust valve on the engine. On one occasion as Alec was taking his sister Hilda for a ride in the sidecar, he had to slow down to go round a corner. Braking into a corner on the BSA was akin to writing a suicide note, so Alec lifted the exhaust valve to slow the engine right down. The whole contraption went up in flames. Alec leaped from the bike, which had come to a sudden halt, and dived over to the other side to grab Hilda. There was a tonneau cover protecting her from the elements, and he couldn't get it undone quickly enough along the side to get her out. Just seconds before the sidecar went up in flames too, he managed to drag her out over the back.

The debacle happened right outside Leichhardt Fire Station. The men emerged in a flash to put out the fire — and have a bit of a laugh besides. Everyone gathered around the smouldering bike, wondering what had happened.

The BSA had a tap in the bottom of the petrol tank. This tap adjoined a priming tap in the top of the cylinder, so that the rider could switch both taps on and put petrol straight into the engine, making the bike easier to start. It also made it easy to really give it to the BSA if speed was needed. The trouble, it seemed, was that the tap in the petrol tank had decided to work itself loose, allowing the petrol to run out all over the engine.

The BSA survived, though Hilda now thought motorbikes were dangerous things. But never so dangerous as in the hands of Walter Bird. Walter, who was later to marry Alec's sister Una, sometimes borrowed the BSA. On the first such occasion he went for a spin around the block in Leichhardt, only to find that he didn't know how to stop. By now accustomed to the BSA's idiosyncrasies, the men at the fire station dropped what they were doing, grabbed the hoses, and came out to watch. And clap. The kids on the block all stopped what they were doing too, and decided to encourage Walter by yelling out 'Here he comes again!' in a chorus each time he came into view. Eventually he managed to stop — when the petrol ran out. That took quite some time.

Alec continued to work a good deal of overtime and was soon able to buy a block of land. The block had a 30-foot frontage, at five pounds a foot, so the total cost was £150. Only the frontage was quoted when land was put up for sale, because the 'per foot' cost took into account the depth of the block. Alec's land was very uneven; a lot of heavy rocks had to be dug up and removed, and others repositioned. Alec made a sledge out of a sheet of corrugated roofing iron, rolled the rocks onto it, and dragged them to their new spot. Hard work, but it had to be done.

He now learned that he could get the 30-foot block next door, for four pounds ten a foot, which would allow him to build a pair of semi-detached cottages — one of which he could let. He had to borrow a lot of money, and pay interest on first and second mortgages. To cut the costs, he did all the electric work, painting, paths and fencing in his 'spare' time. The building contract dictated that the construction had to be finished within six weeks. The cost was £1400. Alec had to admit to himself that he'd been a little extravagant with the design. For a start, he'd wanted bullseye windows — they were the fashion, after all.

Alec and Effie Griffiths moved into their three-quarters-finished home in Segenhoe Street, Arncliffe, around the middle of 1922. The fresh smell of wood and varnish greeted them as Effie was carried over the threshold. There were only two other houses in the area. The rest was paddocks overlooking the tin shed and grass strips of Mascot aerodrome, from which regular air services would start two years later. Alec found it pretty tough going to get his portion of the work finished and to ensure that the builder got his final payments, but by burning the midnight oil he managed somehow.

With the building project out of the way, he now made enough money to bring Effie's family out from Scotland, something she dearly wanted. Effie's sister Alice opted to cross the Tasman and settle in New Zealand, but Alec found a house for the rest of the Melville clan in Arncliffe, just up the road. Adding to Effie's pleasure,

Preserved Western Front trenches and dugouts as they are today. In 1917, any trees had been completely blown clear. (photo Andrew Crack)

Tyne Cot Commonwealth War Cemetery near Passchendaele, Belgium – the final resting place of nearly 12 000 men (photo Andrew Crack)

Alec and Effie, 5 November 1921

Alec's first box-type caravan, self-designed and built

Left to right: Jim, Nancy, Beryl and Bettie

The Griffiths family in 1932 – left to right: Bettie, Effie, Jim, Alec, Beryl, Nancy

Alec Griffiths was the first man to put a caravan on the back of a truck. He registered the design in 1957 (below) but his ingenuity was destined to be unrewarded.

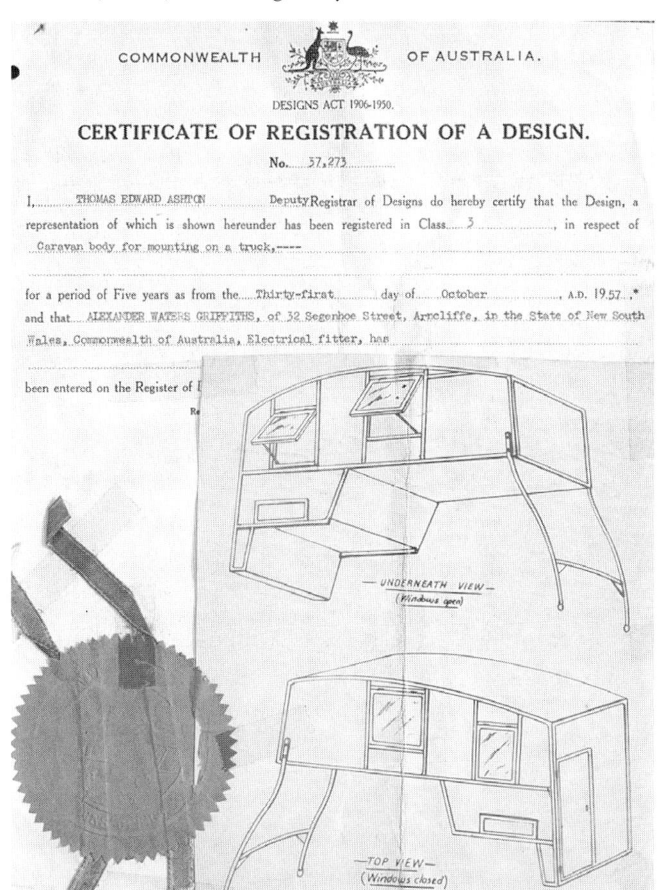

COMMONWEALTH OF AUSTRALIA.

DESIGNS ACT 1906-1950.

CERTIFICATE OF REGISTRATION OF A DESIGN.

No. 37,273

I, THOMAS EDWARD ASHTON Deputy Registrar of Designs do hereby certify that the Design, a representation of which is shown hereunder has been registered in Class 3, in respect of Caravan body for mounting on a truck,----

for a period of Five years as from the Thirty-first day of October, A.D. 1957,* and that ALEXANDER WATERS GRIFFITHS, of 32 Segenhoe Street, Arncliffe, in the State of New South Wales, Commonwealth of Australia, Electrical fitter, has

been entered on the Register of [illegible]

The Griffiths family at Jim's wedding, January 1954. Left to right: Beryl, Bettie, Alec, Effie, Jim and Nancy.

Alec and Effie, Sydney Airport, February 1968, en route to a holiday in New Zealand. This is the last picture of Effie taken before her death in New Zealand one week later.

Alec becomes the centre of attention on his return to the Western Front in 1993 (photo courtesy of Murray Olds)

her first child, dear little Nancy, was born in October. The arrival of such a beautiful, innocent creature helped Alec put the unspeakable things he had seen in the war to the back of his mind. But he couldn't forget them, especially when the first wireless broadcasts began in Australia and brought back memories of using a crystal set in very different circumstances.

Looking after young Nancy occupied much of Alec's time when he wasn't at work, yet he found the time to design and build a box-type trailer, able to be towed behind a car, that would allow him and Effie to get away from Sydney and out into the bush at weekends. But he had to borrow a car to tow it. For Alec, the invention was the beginning of a love affair with camping.

Nancy's lovely new sister, Bettie, was born in September 1924, a year in which regular outings became a way of life for the young family. Alec reckoned he owed it to himself to see a bit more of his country, having survived the tragedies of France and Belgium. After the Western Front, going away to the bush or the beach — Dee Why perhaps, if you wanted both — was the sweetest thing on earth. And it was all happening in a country that was on the up and up. There was a widespread feeling that Australians were creating a society of good values, of hard work, close family bonds, and mateship. Australia was just about the best place a bloke could ever hope to find himself. Of that, Alec was certain.

But there were changes everywhere. A big bank was being constructed at the top of Martin Place — one of the first multistorey buildings in Sydney. In the midst of a building boom, this town was slowly but surely pushing itself into the big league. And the thing that was doing all the pushing was concrete. Whenever he looked at the streetscapes Alec had to pinch himself to remember that it was the same town he had left behind in 1916. On all the building sites around Sydney concrete was being mixed on the job in small concrete mixers. Ready-mix concrete? Not on your life, not in 1925. The streets were noisy with the machines' churning and grinding, and cement dust blended with progress to fill the air. Especially in summer, in heat that would buckle railway lines, the last thing you wanted was to breath cement dust. But what could you do? Sydney had taken it upon itself to leave behind the days of sandstone edifices graced by shady wooden-post verandahs. It had chosen to pay the price of becoming a city of the world.

To drive the concrete mixers the builders had to have electric motors, which required a fair amount of maintenance. As well, the builders had powered hoists which were used like lifts, and they required maintenance also. And wherever electrical maintenance was needed, Alec could get work. He was given a sub-contracting job on the Martin Place site until the bank's completion. His own employer ran a non-union outfit, as he didn't believe in unions. 'Pack o' whingers', he called them. But when some bloke at the unionised site got wind of the fact that Alec wasn't in a union, he gave the project boss an ultimatum: 'Make Griffiths a union member or we all go on strike. We'll stop the job.' The site workers didn't have any particular hostility towards Alec; it was just that the union organisers knew a political instrument when they saw one. So Alec joined the Electrical Trades Union — which not only kept him his job at the Martin Place site but made it easier for him to take on other work in the years ahead.

* * *

The year 1926 saw the birth of the Griffiths' third daughter, Beryl, a little charmer who became known as Billie. Her parents had not for one moment considered that they might have another girl. Consequently, girls' names had never entered any conversation.

'What are you going to call her?' the matron at the hospital enquired.

'We don't know,' Alec replied.

'We've only thought of "Billy", for a boy,' Effie added.

'Well,' the matron said, 'you can still call her Billie. Billie's a lovely name for a girl.' And so Billie she became, despite being christened Beryl. She was destined to be the beauty of the family, and this showed from the minute she was born.

That was also the year Alec's brother Fred settled down to life on dry land. He had been at sea almost continuously since 1915 and had seen more of the world in those years than most people do in two lifetimes. He took a job as a senior telegraphist with AWA.

And he bought Alec an ice-cream.

1926 was also the year for Going Away. In December, after crossing the Georges River by punt and making their way down past all the farms, Alec and Effie took a humble cottage called 'Bright', at Gunnamatta Bay, Cronulla. The house would thereafter be taken each year and many members of the extended family would join them. 'Bright' was right on the beach. With the tide out there were stretches of muddy sand, forever carpeted in an advancing — or retreating — army of small soldier crabs. In the gaps between the advancing battalions, Alec and Hilda's husband Cal would take up their guns and charge in. The crabs weren't too concerned. The guns were yabby guns; but their targets were sandworms. When they weren't going after worms the two brothers-in-law just dug with their hands for pipis.

A small rowing boat belonged to 'Bright', and on a lazy Saturday afternoon that first year Alec and Cal and a couple of others took out a few lines and some bait they'd collected, with the intention of catching a fish or two. Since Cal had never been out in a boat before, and had never caught a fish in his life, he was the butt of some good-natured ribbing.

As it turned out, though, he was the only one to catch anything, so he had the last laugh. When the fish were brought home, Gran Griffiths refused to waste a thing. Her early years — as Eliza Jane Griffiths of 'Shaftsbury' — had taught her that. As well as cooking the fish for the meal she made soup from the fish heads. This was not altogether a popular decision, but Gran Griffiths declared that nobody would get anything else to eat until each soup bowl was so clean they could see their reflection in it.

Entertainment in the evening relied on an old wind-up gramophone and a number of records. One set of records featured a comedian called Casey: 'Casey at the Races', 'Casey at the Beach', 'Casey in Court', and so on. In 'Casey in Court, the judge questioning him asked, 'Do you eat onions?'

'No,' Casey replied.

The judge then asked, 'Does your brother eat onions?'

'I don't have a brother.'

'If you did have a brother, would he eat onions?'

This particular exchange never failed to bring howls of laughter from the assembled listeners.

On the Monday, the family members who were part of the workforce and hadn't been able to arrange their holidays to coincide with the stay at 'Bright' had to go to work. Once the tide had gone out they walked along the sand to Cronulla, where they could catch a bus or tram to their destination. This year Alec was one of them. Most of the waterfront houses he passed along the way featured brightly coloured nasturtiums, which trailed over the sea walls and spilled onto the sand. Alec remembered the colourless landscape of Flanders, and smiled. He whistled a tune all the way to Cronulla.

* * *

In 1928 Alec, Effie and their family walked down to Mascot aerodrome to welcome Bert Hinkler after he made the first solo flight from England. It would be the last time they had to walk any great distance to get somewhere, for 1928 was the year in which Alec purchased the first car that he didn't have to work on and then sell to make money. It was a case of 'with the kids came the car'. A six-cylinder Studebaker touring car with great long running boards, it was a sight to behold, even though it wasn't new. The Studie only had rear brakes. The windscreen wiper was hand-operated. And the tail light had its own switch, so Alec had to get out of the car when dusk fell and switch the bugger on. It had a collapsible roof of waterproof material, but it was a devil of a job to get the roof back up. The trigger for rolling it open was a day so hot that tyres with their 60 pounds of pressure were starting to melt into the road.

Alec built a large platform on the back of the car, which allowed Effie and him to carry a motheaten tent, a canvas watercooler bag and other camping gear when they went on holiday. He also fitted a hinged partition onto one of the running boards, and this they could shove all their luggage behind. Digger, their young blue cattle dog, rode on the other running board, displaying superb balance.

One of the Griffithses' favourite camping spots was Kangaroo Valley. This was also much liked by the two grandmas, who often joined the family on weekends away. The main feature of Kangaroo Valley wasn't 'roos; it was rabbits. When Alec went outside at dusk, the entire hillside would appear to be moving as a vast carpet of rabbits did their best to strip it clear of vegetation. A shot fired anywhere into the hillside was certain to bring down a prize. Taking aim was unnecessary.

Alec still didn't like using a gun, but one or two locals would stop by and give them a few carcasses. Consequently there would always be a huge pot of rabbit stew simmering on the campfire, to be washed down with liberal portions of billy tea. Living off rabbit stew at Kangaroo Valley made for a most economical weekend holiday. And there was no need to pay money for the site. It was the 1920s: you could just pull off the side of the road — anywhere at all — and camp.

CHAPTER NINETEEN
Segenhoe Street

Across the road from Alec's place there lived a boy called Cobber. Bettie and Cobber were great mates, and they could always find some mischief which appealed to them. One day, without telling anyone of their intentions, they set off together on a Dinky tricycle and a toy car — which they shared — seeking adventure. They sped off down the hill, climbed onto a path which went along the top of a new sewer pipe, and kept going. After a long journey they found themselves, confused and worn-out, on the tram tracks in front of the swimming baths at Brighton-le-Sands. Their disappearance sparked an expansive search, and eventually one of the searchers, Cobber's father in his horse-drawn sulky, found them and brought them to justice. When Bettie was dropped back at home, it was made clear to her — crystal clear — that there had best not be a repetition of this escapade.

And of this incident there was no repetition, but it was far from the last mischief she got herself tangled up in. Down the street a bit there lived a lady known to the local kids as Pearly. Bettie and the other kids knew her as quite an eccentric lady, who had never married, appeared to have no family and lived alone. She was also known as 'the cat lady' because she befriended every stray cat in

Arncliffe. Her house was full of them. Not only was she the butt of the local kids' taunts, but they also frequented her garden to pinch the fruit straight off the trees. 'I know it's you Griffiths kids out there!' she'd scream from the security of her living room. 'I know by your red hair!'

The striking redhead of the family, Bettie had fire in her soul to match. She was also the one the local boys taunted, with labels of 'carrots' and 'copper-top'. 'What made the donkey buck?' they teased. 'Carrots?' came her reluctant yet haughty reply. 'No. Ginger!' they countered, and pulled her hair. The story was related back to her father. Alec had expected his daughter to burst into tears. Instead, with a glint in her eye, she grinned. He never found out what she had done to the boys, but they never teased her again; in fact they never showed up in Segenhoe Street again. Even up at the Arncliffe shops, boys her age would cower at the very sight of her. Arncliffe was not a very large suburb and word got around easily.

Despite its small population, Arncliffe one day in 1930 seemed like the most populous place on earth. Thousands gathered in the vicinity of Segenhoe Street — which had perhaps the most commanding view of Mascot in Sydney — to watch the landing of aviatrix Amy Johnson. Even young Nancy watched the end of Johnson's history-making flight from England, from her grandstand seat: the playground at Arncliffe Primary School. That day Nan was only one of thousands of very impressed little Australian girls.

It was also in 1930 that Effie gave birth to the Griffithses' only son, christened James but known to all as Jim. Effie and Alec seriously wondered whether they could survive the Great Depression — which had now set in — with yet another mouth to feed. But they were doing well enough and were determined to be thankful for what they did have, rather than be unthankful for what they didn't. Many people were worse off than they, after all. There were a lot of people living in humpies at Botany Bay. Anywhere there was vacant land there were people squatting. A lot of them were on susso. But the government didn't want to hand out too much in the way of sustenance payments or relief because it reckoned that, if it did, nobody would want to seek work.

Huge numbers were evicted because they couldn't pay their rent. The irony of it was that thousands remained homeless while houses stood vacant. When people saw these empty houses they often took the law into their own hands and squatted there. Things got so bad during the Depression that at one point, in June 1931, there was almost a revolution. They called that day Bloody Friday. Alec couldn't believe that things had got so bad in a country that had fought so hard for freedom and a peaceful, prosperous way of life. But they had.

Fortunately, Alec and Effie never had to apply for food coupons. Nonetheless, they didn't have it all that easy. Alec was still working for Coupland & Waddell, and while the firm didn't give anyone the sack, if no jobs came in the men didn't get paid. For weeks at a time Alec endured going into work, finding no jobs, and going home. He still had to pay his train fare in the morning and at night. But there was no money coming into Segenhoe Street, so the young Griffiths family had to live off the little that Alec could borrow.

He had been adventurous in the first place by building not one but two cottages. This would have been perfectly all right had the Depression not come on. But fortunately for Alec a very kind man, Mr Curtis, held the mortgage. When it came time for Alec to make the mortgage payments he would say, 'Oh, never mind about that for the moment, Alec. And if you need any extra money, you can have it without interest.' That was the only thing that got the young family through the Depression, although Alec's brother Lock also helped in small ways. Lock now worked at the Customs Department and it was his job to board visiting ships and inspect them. He'd become pretty friendly with the cooks on the ships, and every now and again he'd bring Effie a leg of ham or something like that — something that Alec could never have afforded in a million years.

Of course, they never went completely hungry: 'bread and milk' — whereby bread was cut into squares, doused in sugar and soaked in milk — was frequently on offer. Effie always had a big pot of vegetable soup on the stove. Even if that was all the Griffiths family had to eat for days on end, they remembered the people in the humpies along the shores of Botany Bay. Some of these people spent all their time gathering seashells, which they crushed by hand with rocks and sold as shell grit for poultry feed. Some made shell necklaces and bangles too, but sales were rare. At La Perouse, Aborigines dived for the occasional coin thrown into the water by a passer-by. The passer-by got entertained, the diver got the coin. Out past Kurnell, Aborigines charmed snakes and threw boomerangs to try and earn a few bob. The trouble was, scarcely anyone in Sydney had a bob to spare.

Other men 'went on the wallaby' — moving around to all the properties in the bush looking for work. All they had to their name were their belongings in a swag. If they didn't get work (which was usually the case) at least they might get a meal; otherwise they lived off nothing but damper for weeks on end. Alec had a few mates who, in desperation, left Sydney to give it a go in the bush. Most of them blew back in, saying it was even worse out there.

Clothing for the family was Alec's main concern. With the scarcity of money, not only because of the Depression but because of the mortgage, every penny available for the purchase of clothes called for the utmost wisdom in its use. Clothing was the thing that hit people the most. If you didn't eat, there was always tomorrow. But clothes? Another story entirely.

There was a bloke called the Remnant Man who came to the door every now and again selling oblong pieces of material with holes in them for arms and neck. Each piece cost a shilling, and Effie would make a few dresses out of it for the girls. Tremendous excitement accompanied the visit by the Remnant Man, for any purchases made determined the Griffithses' wardrobe for the next six months or so. Other than that, the young girls might have to be content with hessian sacks with holes cut in them — a very different sight from the dresses worn by children from the affluent families of Sydney, dresses with their huge puffed sleeves and frilly skirts.

Alec and Effie knew that their own daughters were conscious of the difference but there was little they could do about it. So they 'spent' in other ways: they spent time, precious family time. They all stayed happy, with singsongs around the old piano (Effie couldn't read a note of music but she could play anything by ear!), and reading Ginger Meggs comics together. Alec and Effie listened to the wireless in the evenings, as it seldom broadcast during the day: the Australian National Orchestra and various dance bands on 2FC; the comedienne Peggy Pryde on 2BL. And once a year Effie and her mother trekked into the big sales at the department stores to buy each of the girls a plain overcoat. These coats were the girls' entire 'warm garment' wardrobe for the year, yet the love that lay behind their purchase meant they could have been diamond-studded furs. Nan, Bettie and Billie were always over the moon when the coats were unwrapped.

Another visitor to the street, who often came around in the evenings, was 'the Rabbito Man'. A big lanky bloke, he walked down the road chanting 'Rabbito! Rabbito!' as he went. Out of the house the Griffiths children raced, eager to catch him at the front gate. He had rabbits, tied by the back legs in pairs, and carried these bundles over his shoulders. They cost one shilling and sixpence per pair. If you asked him he'd skin them for you, a simple job for him. He just ran his knife around each rabbit's neck and legs and pulled off the skin in one go. In these days before myxomatosis disease was introduced to deal with the rabbit numbers threatening the Australian countryside, rabbit stew was a particularly nice if uncommon treat. The Rabbito Man didn't make very much from so much hard work, but he was doing his best to make a quid.

There was another voice the family heard from time to time. It belonged to a chap who came along Segenhoe Street calling out 'Clothes props! Clothes props!' at the top of his voice. He spent half of his time out in the bush cutting down saplings, which he would trim until he finished up with a pole about eight feet long with a fork at the top. The other half of his time he spent wandering the streets of Sydney selling the product. Clothes props were used by housewives to stop the clothes line sagging when wet clothes were hung out to dry.

The only unwelcome visitors were the bedbugs. The blighters sensed hardship, and were a horrible nuisance. Making the bed in the morning, you'd look for fleas and bedbugs; you'd search all through the sheets, and if there were bloody spots you knew they'd got you in the night. The pain was a pretty sure indication, too. Secure and smug in their shells, the bedbugs were like incredibly small turtles, only nowhere near as innocuous. Like ladybirds with all the colour sucked out of them and replaced with evil. Pure evil. They worked their way all through the bed — through the woodwork, through the coils. They reminded Alec of the vermin in Flanders. They even worked themselves through the floorboards of the house.

Alec declared war. He took all the bedsprings outside, poured kero all over them and set them alight. This solved the bedbug problem for a while, but then more bedbugs would decide it was time to move house — from another house in the same street. Segenhoe Street now had its fair share of houses, and there were plenty of dogs around who unwittingly acted as removal lorries. True, fly-tox was beaut for killing blowflies, but it was impotent against the might of bedbugs and fleas. There was a saying around Sydney, vouching that people in the slums had bedbugs, while people in the better suburbs had fleas. Somehow, Segenhoe Street got cursed with both.

* * *

Jack Lang, the premier of New South Wales, felt that the whole Depression in Australia had been aggravated, if not brought on, by British bankers. During Lang's second period in office, in the early 1930s, Alec couldn't get any money from the banks, because Lang's actions had virtually shut them down. As part of a political battle with the federal government, the premier had withdrawn State funds from the banks. Everybody was panicking and saying, 'If the banks go broke, Australia goes broke, and there will be no more Australia.' Many people withdrew their own money. As the banks didn't have enough funds it made things pretty difficult, as people were very hard up anyway. In 1932 the state governor, Sir Phillip Game, stepped in and dismissed Lang from office. Having helped to put the whole country in turmoil, Lang lost the subsequent election.

Alec wouldn't have called Jack Lang good or bad as a premier. It all depended on how you judged a man. Lang had a job to do under difficult circumstances; tough decisions had to be made, and he made them. He had the Depression working against him and consequently the people turned against him. But Alec felt he was a people's politician. He didn't get driven to work in a flash car or live in a flash house. In fact he lived on the opposite side of the street to Alec's sister-in-law in Schofield, and very often he'd travel into town on the train with her.

On 19 March 1932, before his dismissal, Lang — well, Captain de Groot and then Lang — officially opened the Sydney Harbour Bridge. Alec and Effie had been watching it go up since 1923 and had often wondered whether the two halves of the structure growing out from the harbour sides would ever actually be joined. And if they were, whether they would meet evenly. The two halves had been anchored by steel cables, and to finish up the builders had to release the cables and let the two halves come together. The builders were fortunate in that the weather was good on the big day. The calculations were exact. And the bridge just dropped into position without any trouble. Alec was there to see it. In a sense it gave the people hope. They had lived through war and were amid the Depression, and the bridge somehow symbolised a bright future for Australia. For Alec, it was wonderful to see that iron and steel — the evil elements used in the pulverising machines of war — were being employed in such a way.

Crossing the bridge was a novelty the Griffiths family looked forward to; being able to say you'd crossed it as a pedestrian on the day it was opened was a big thing. To say you'd driven across it on the day they opened the roadway was even bigger. Before they built the bridge there was no way to get across the harbour except by a vehicular ferry located at almost the same spot. The ferry didn't follow cables like most punts. It had to be steered through a terrific current that ran through the narrow part of the harbour there, so they had built special landing barriers which were very wide to start off with and which got narrower as the ferry went in further. They were designed in effect to 'funnel' the ferry into its berth. For years the ferries had relied upon kerosene lights for illumination. Alec had had the job of fitting electric lights in them, one of the most unpleasant jobs he'd ever had to do. The ex-military generators had to go in the tiny space below deck in the bilges, where there was nothing but oil and slush. He was glad when the job was done.

Other symbols, too, kept the nation going through the Depression. Everyone looked forward to Empire Day, a very important day in the Australian calendar — especially for the kids, who got half a day off school. At morning assembly they stood at attention as the flag was raised and recited, 'I honour my God, I serve my King, I salute my flag', and would then be lectured about the British Empire and sing all the patriotic songs. For weeks prior, the kids practised singing the patriotic songs they'd practised for weeks: songs such as 'Land of Hope and Glory', 'Three Cheers for the Red, White and Blue' and 'There'll Always Be An England'. 'See all these red bits on the map?' the teachers would ask. 'They all belong to the British Empire. And the sun *never* sets on the Empire.' The kids would be given Australian flags or Union Jacks and then gather at the local picture theatre dressed in their best clothes to sing to their mums and dads and wave the little flags.

Their afternoon would be spent playing games such as skipping, hide and seek, marbles and hopscotch. At least at this time of year the hopscotch squares could be drawn in chalk on the road. In midsummer, when the kids tried to draw the squares, the hot tar disintegrated the chalk and they would have to content themselves with bursting the hot tar blisters instead. Empire Day would end with cracker night. All the kids in the Arncliffe area would bring bits of wood to Segenhoe Street for weeks before the big night, in preparation for the bonfire the Griffithses always lit in the laneway behind the house. The only member of the family who didn't enjoy the fireworks was Digger, who spent the night cowering under the house wishing it was all over.

After the Great Depression finally ended, Uncle Cal took up the position of postmaster at Bungendore, near Canberra, but the two families still kept up with each other. Many a time the Griffithses would head down there for the Christmas holiday. And Cal and Hilda and their family continued to come up to Arncliffe to stay with them.

They were good days. Food became more readily available and services improved again. The milkman came along in his cart everyday, drawn by a horse. The milkman had a big tank on the back of the cart, with a tap at the end. The kids had to take a billycan out to him and hold it underneath the tap while the milkman measured out the milk. Young Jim, however, didn't always wait for the milkman to arrive to 'get' his milk. Quite the scallywag, he was often up to some prank or other. One of these, which brought the police to Segenhoe Street to have a stern word with his parents, concerned a small dairy farm at the bottom of the hill, tucked in between the Chinese gardens and the 'stink pipe' and overlooked by the house. Alec and Effie learned from the police that three or four lads, including their son, frequented the dairy farm where each would claim a cow. Each boy would then proceed to use 'their' cow as a water pistol — or rather a 'milk pistol' — by squirting milk at each other straight from the cows' teats. Naturally these shenanigans were not looked upon favourably by the dairy farmer, and even less so by the cows themselves.

For a time, the butcher paid a regular delivery visit to Segenhoe Street. He'd often stay a while, talking about anything and everything. One of his visits coincided with the arrival in the household of a new litter of puppies, a mixture of blue cattle dog (from Digger) and fox terrier (from Digger's 'wife' Trixie). Having fox terrier in their breeding, it seemed that shortening their tails was the correct thing to do. The butcher fancied himself as quite the expert on dogs, and so was very flattered, pleased and puffed up with self-importance when Alec and Effie sought his advice on what to do. 'Leave it to me,' he offered airily. And with that he grabbed the puppies one by one, in very quick succession, and bit off each of their tails and spat them out. The family could only look on with revulsion and disbelief. The kids never let him near the house again, and thereafter Effie exercised great caution on the few occasions she bought meat.

The baker, on the other hand, was most welcome. He also came around with a horse and cart, delivering bread that was still warm and that cost between thruppence and sixpence a loaf. Since the bread was unwrapped, you could smell the priceless aroma of freshly baked dough even before the cart arrived at the gate. A tin loaf was the prized item. In reality it was two loaves which you'd have to pull apart. One side was just squared-off bread, where it had rested in the tin during baking. The other side was blackened crust, where it had swollen up and got the heat on it so much it became completely charred. Alec and Effie seldom got to eat much of the good part; the kids would have pulled the two halves apart in the short distance between the baker's cart and the house, and the warm, spongy bread inside the crust would be gone by the time they got to the front door.

Alec could now afford to keep a few chickens in the backyard, which were kept for Christmas dinners and special occasions. First he had to run around the yard and catch the chook, then cut off its head and plunge it into the boiling water of the huge gas copper on the back verandah. By leaving it there for quite some time the theory was that this would loosen the feathers. In practice they were still stuck like glue and took hours to pluck. Gutting the chook was Alec's responsibility, while Effie made the stuffing from scratch and the kids shelled the peas. After the meal the greasy copper had to be cleaned out. As it was fixed, it couldn't just be tipped out. Alec cleaned as much as he could reach, but more often than not one of the kids would have to get inside it once the water had been drained, and clean the bottom of it. Christmas Dinner took half a day to prepare and a whole day to clean up after, but the work involved made them most appreciative of the meal. The only real downside of the whole procedure was that the family's clothes, no matter how much Sapolene and Blue Bags were used to wash and rinse them in the gas copper, would smell of chicken for weeks afterwards.

These were also the halcyon years of lamingtons, homemade chips and Anzac biscuits. A day with chips followed by fudge made with condensed milk from the cupboard was considered a day in heaven. Now and again Effie would send the kids up to the Arncliffe shops for a pound of minced steak and a kidney. At fivepence for the meat and a penny for the kidney this didn't happen all that often, but when it did, Effie cooked it up and mixed it with soup vegetables. It was bonzer!

PART IV

WORLD WAR II AND BEYOND

CHAPTER TWENTY
At War Again

It is my melancholy duty to inform you officially that in consequence of a persistence by Germany in her invasion of Poland, Great Britain has declared war upon her and that, as a result, Australia is also at war.

Prime Minister Robert Gordon Menzies

The Griffithses had to say goodbye to their old Studebaker when Alec started having to go out and collect faulty electric motors for repair. They were too big to fit in the car. In its place he bought a ten horsepower Bedford truck. They still went camping frequently, especially around Nelligen, but the caravan they now used was soon replaced by one another of Alec's inventions. He'd wondered why you would tow a caravan behind a truck when you could sit it on the truck and tow a boat as well. And so he built a small boat — a clinker-built one — and in his workshop at Segenhoe Street he designed and constructed a 'caravan' to be bolted on the tray of the truck. His boss at Coupland & Waddell got him to paint the firm's name on the side of the 'cara-ute'. Alec then charged them for the times he had to pick up a big motor, bring it in for repairs and then take it back again, so it suited him too. It was a good business relationship, and Alec's position with the firm was more satisfying than ever.

September of that year, 1939, started quietly enough. On the third day, during a delicious spring evening when the family were sitting as usual around the wireless, listening or having a yarn, they suddenly heard the voice of Robert Menzies, the Australian prime minister. It began by saying, 'It is my melancholy duty...' and went on to inform listeners that Australia was at war.

Effie was horrified. The kids were speechless. And Alec's nose suddenly began to bleed profusely. Menzies had not even put it to the Australian people! He'd simply decided that Australia was at war, now that Britain was. Just like that. Alec knew what war meant. The shock of knowing it had started again was too much. He had never had a nosebleed up to that point, and never would again.

In the following days and weeks, men rushed to enlist. Alec was not ashamed that he didn't want to join up again. It would take a rare breed of man who could live through the misery of the Western Front and even consider going to war — any war — a second time. Some of the 1st AIF blokes understated their age and went, but not many. Alec was thankful that his son James was far too young to join up and would be spared the horror of war. Nan, on the other hand, did her bit by joining the Voluntary Aid Detachment at Sydney University, at which she was now doing a science degree. Alec was keen to serve his country in whatever capacity he could, provided it didn't involve being shelled or bombed. That disqualified about 90 per cent of positions in the armed forces, but later on he would be accepted by the Royal Australian Navy as a 'defence civilian' and engage in some highly secret work on ships.

For a time it became known as the 'phoney war'. No one seemed to be taking it too seriously. Soldiers appeared to be more concerned with enjoying themselves than with getting to the war. Occasionally Alec would drive past an Army convoy stopped by the side of the road, Diggers milling all around it. Many of the trucks were leftovers that World War I had not managed to consume, and for Alec their solid rubber tyres brought back memories and, curiously, a wry smile. These older trucks were forever breaking down, as was to be expected, given their vintage. Strangely, though, they always broke down outside a hotel.

Life went on pretty much as normal for everyone. A lot of people weren't keen on the idea of the war to begin with. When Alec learned, in June 1940, of the German destruction of Amiens, and read of the Germans fighting in the area around Poperinghe, he knew it was all fair dinkum and lamented, 'Not again.' Only after Chester Wilmot's broadcasts reached home, bearing news of the besieged Aussie garrison at Tobruk, did other people realise the scale of the war and truly get behind the war effort. In April 1941 the Labor Party declared that it stood alongside Menzies and supported England to the last man and the last machine. Alec remembered the pledge of support for England to the last man and the last shilling a quarter of a century earlier, and seriously doubted whether the politicians had learned anything at all from the Great War.

In 1941 the cruiser HMAS *Sydney* returned after having had a very successful time of things in the Mediterranean. Seemingly the whole of Sydney turned out to welcome the crew home. The sight of sailors marching through the streets and being bestowed with the honour of Freedom of the City made Alec feel — not for the first time in his life — proud to be an Australian. It was a time for celebration. But in November the happiness vanished when the new prime minister, John Curtin, announced the loss of the *Sydney* off the Western Australian coast. The entire complement of 645 officers and men perished when the cruiser went down following an action against a German raider — which was itself sunk by the *Sydney* in the course of the battle. The tragedy brought the war much closer to home. It was a particularly sad day for Alec. Twenty-four years earlier — almost to the very day — his best mate Bob Lauchland had died. He had been 25 years old. Alec wondered how many of the blokes who went down with the *Sydney* had also failed to live beyond the age of 25. And how many of them had been the best mates of someone who would live another 25 years or more.

News now came on the wireless of an enormous number of Allied ships blowing up at sea for no apparent reason. It brought to mind visions of ships' spines snapping, a chilling thought. Eventually the authorities realised that magnetic mines, invented and deployed by the Germans, were the cause. Australia, like the other Allied nations, had to demagnetise its ships. Alec volunteered for service immediately, determined to assist in any way he could to combat the severe loss of shipping. It was known that when iron ships are away from the Equator they have a residual amount of magnetism, and that the further they sail away from the Equator the stronger their magnetic field becomes. The method used to neutralise the magnetic field was known as degaussing, and the work was top secret.

First you had to ascertain how much magnetism a ship had to begin with. This process was carried out at Bradley's Head, where a weather-beaten, instrument-filled old hut looked out over Sydney Harbour. Out on the bottom of the harbour were other instruments. All of them were connected by wires. As soon as a ship passed over, the instruments in the little hut recorded how much magnetism it had. Immediately the chart would go to the Navy, and then straight to Alec to do what the Navy men required in the way of neutralising procedures. These involved encircling the ships with wires which would carry an electric current. Alec's job was to calculate the flow of electricity needed to counteract the magnetism, and to supervise the installation of wires around the ship. In the early days there was no time to put the wires inside the vessel, as the turnaround of troopships and cargo ships carrying supplies to the war was so quick. Instead, the wires were wrapped in canvas and just clipped to the outside of the hull. As each ship steamed out towards the ocean again, Alec waited in the hut on Bradley's Head, checking his instruments to ensure that it had been demagnetised.

In turbulent seas a lot of damage was being caused to the degaussing wires and repairs had to be made for many ships when they returned to Sydney. Eventually the wires were put inside the hull; a devil of a job as holes had to be cut through all the bulkheads.

It was necessary to have a man in almost every cabin, each of them able to handle a bunch of very heavy wires. Every time a ship arrived in Sydney Harbour, Alec trekked down to the Labour Exchange in Erskine Street and picked as many as 40 or 50 men to work on the job.

With all this, and doing the timekeeping for pay purposes, Alec was extremely busy. Often he worked day and night, though he didn't much mind because he'd done the same a quarter of a century earlier, working for his country in World War I. There was one significant difference. The hut on Bradley's Head beat the hell out of a shell-torn dugout surrounded by corpses.

The family seldom saw him, as he generally left before it got light and came home after dark. Even on Christmas Day 1940 he had not been immune from the demands of his job. Just as the family was sitting down to Christmas dinner, there was a telephone call. The Griffithses hadn't had a telephone for long and it startled everyone. Only a few weeks earlier Alec had been quite excited, waiting for it to ring. But nobody had rung. It hadn't occurred to him that no one knew his telephone number. When finally Effie happened to ring him, Alec wondered who the strange Scottish lady on the line was. Her accent was so heightened that he didn't recognise her voice.

There was no such accent with this telephone call on Christmas Day. A nasal Aussie voice said, 'There's a speedboat waitin' fer y'at Circular Quay, to take y'over to the *Queen* bloody *Mary*. There's somethin' wrong with the degaussing. Quick as y' can, Griffo!' But before Alec could leave he had to light up the gas producer on his little truck. This was a charcoal-burning device used to power vehicles because of the wartime shortage of petrol. It took quite a while to get it going properly. Eventually he arrived at Circular Quay.

Down on the harbour the *Queen Mary*, painted grey for camouflage and with her portholes blackened out with paint, was moored with two anchor chains out for'ard. As the ship had swung a lot in the wind, the chains had got twisted together. A tug had been enlisted to tow the stern of the enormous ship around and around in order to take the twists out of the chains. It must have been quite a sight: the majestic *Queen Mary* spinning around slowly just inside the Heads, without actually going anywhere. Then the tow rope from the tug had caught under the degaussing wires and pulled them all off. Panic had followed, because the ship was loaded with troops and ready to go to sea. To make matters worse, it had a rendezvous to keep with other ships outside the Heads which all had to go off in convoy.

Alec had to go ashore and ring up as many of the workers as he could on a Christmas Day, and bring them out urgently to get the job done. Already they'd lost time because Alec had to get his confounded gas producer going. The *Queen Mary* was enormous — you needed a motorcycle just to get from one end of the ship to the other. After working for days and nights, the lads got the job done. They couldn't do the whole ship, otherwise it would never have got away; other sections had to be installed at other ports. But they got enough degaussing wires in place to ensure reasonable safety from magnetic mines. Finally the *Queen Mary* left on 28 December. And Alec never again had trouble getting petrol for his truck. The Navy saw to that.

* * *

When the Griffithses heard in February 1942 that Darwin had been bombed, there was a feeling of absolute despair, and along with it the inevitable feeling of 'thank goodness it wasn't us'. People weren't told all that much about it, and while Alec reckoned there was probably a bit of a cover-up with respect to how many people were actually killed, he reasoned that the authorities had to make sure the rest of Australia didn't panic. Not much was said of the damage to Darwin owing to censorship in the press, but in the last war Alec had become adept at reading between the lines of censorship and propaganda, and guessed the human toll to be far worse than admitted. Nonetheless, despite the dearth of information regarding the bombing, everyone had the wind up; there was a feeling of helplessness because they didn't have much protection against that sort of thing. As at Pearl Harbor, it was a very savage attack. In fact more Japanese planes pummelled poor old Darwin than had hit the Americans at Pearl Harbor, and yet it was being hushed up.

The war came much closer to the Griffiths family a few months later. At the end of May, three Japanese midget submarines came into Sydney Harbour. One of them torpedoed the *Kuttabul*, which had been used as a depot ship, and some nineteen men were killed. Two of the submarines, at least, came to grief. A lot of people reckoned the Japs were actually after the cruiser *Chicago*, one of a number of US Navy ships in the harbour at the time. After that incident many people wanted the American ships out of Sydney because they made it a more important target than it really was. The sight of the *Kuttabul*, which had been sunk in shallow water at Woolloomooloo, was tragic. Alec was seeing something on his doorstep — in his beloved, jewelled city of Sydney — that he had sworn he would never see again. He was seeing *war*.

Not long after the submarine attack the Japanese shelled a few of Sydney's beachside suburbs. There wasn't a lot of damage but it frightened people. Houses became vacant along the coast — especially around Bondi and Coogee — because their owners had moved up to the mountains. A submarine net was strung across Port Hacking River just south of Cronulla. The old holiday spot, where lazy, peaceful summer days had been whiled away not so long ago, was now at risk of enemy attack. Another net cordoned off Georges River, at Bald Face Point. How could they be getting so close?

Although people in general tried to carry on their lives more or less as normal, there was considerable nervousness in the air. Singapore, the Far Eastern Naval Base of the Royal Navy, had been the bulwark against invading hordes. The Griffiths family, for one, had been confident that Britain wouldn't let Australians down. After all, the Aussies had helped the Poms during the Great War, in the Dardanelles, in Mesopotamia and on the Western Front. And not only had Australia sent its boys over to Mother England to help defend her in the Battle of Britain in 1940, it had sent whole battalions of Diggers to the Middle East as well.

But Singapore had fallen, early in 1942. Thousands of Diggers had been captured by the Japanese. The path to invasion of Australia had been blazed as though with a scythe.

CHAPTER TWENTY-ONE

Over (T)here, Over (T)here

American servicemen began to appear on the streets, in large numbers. They were far more glamorous than the Australian men, and had far more money to spend. They paid less for their smokes than Australian soldiers did. Altogether they *seemed* more worldly wise. Once you got talking to some of them, though, you thought quite the opposite. A lot of local girls reckoned that Australian blokes were 'Dad and Dave' types compared to the Americans — the Yanks looked so much better in their uniforms. That much was obvious. Australian uniforms were often of different shades, having come from different factories, whereas the Yanks' uniforms were tailor-made. What a turnaround from the last war, Alec thought. In 1917 a slouch-hatted Australian lad in a Light Horse or Flying Corps uniform was a prize much sought after by the ladies. Now, a quarter of a century later, the poor old slouch hat couldn't hold a candle to the Americans' smart forage caps in the eyes of the girls. Especially when the candle was gleaming on a dining table in a flash restaurant, next to a bottle of champagne.

To the girls such as Nancy Griffiths only a few years earlier, 'GI' had meant 'geographically impossible': if a young man lived too far away from Arncliffe, he was 'GI', and no matter how handsome he was, he would be struck off the list of potential suitors. Now, GI meant something completely different. The Yanks really seemed to know what the girls wanted, and got them going in a fluster. Armed with nylon stockings, perfumes and other rarities, the visitors won many victories with little need for basic strategy. Alec saw the charm offensive in the streets of Sydney every day. Australians were living a life in which petrol, clothing, tea, butter and even sugar were rationed ... and there were the Americans with their bottles of champagne and nylon stockings. Nylons hadn't been thought of in Australia. Stockings were silk, they laddered if you so much as looked at them and they had to be mended. You couldn't just throw them away, they cost a fortune. There were even shops that specialised in the invisible mending of laddered stockings. Once a woman's very last pair had died, she might use leg paint instead, including a painted seam up the back of the leg. The only trouble with this system was that the brown paint came off as soon as Sydney got humid, which was most days of the year.

The Yanks also had their own 'canteens' at which they would lay out a huge spread for dinner and put on a dance. Bettie and Beryl often went along as hostesses. By doing this, Beryl, whose beauty as a very young girl called 'Billie' had continued through her teens, aroused Alec's protective instincts. With her golden, wavy hair and model's figure she presented herself in the early evening, ready to head off, and became most indignant when her father asked her to remove some of her lipstick.

He needn't have been so protective. Both sisters one day brought an American soldier home as a friend. His name was Elmer and he had a Purple Heart award, which he made quite a lot of. The family were very impressed until they realised that all wounded American soldiers got the Purple Heart — Alec reckoned a lot of them must have got it for cutting their finger or stubbing a toe. But Elmer was a nice enough boy and the family liked him.

Quite a few Australian girls who fell for the visitors, however, came a cropper later. The Yanks were really able to put on a turn and pass themselves off as landed gentry, and when the girls went off to the United States aboard the special 'bride ships' many of them found they were lucky even to have a roof over their heads. Expecting to be the head of the manor, some actually ended up being slave of the manor. Marriages fell apart very quickly. Once news of this got back to Australia, a lot of Aussie soldiers reckoned these girls had got what they deserved.

A favourite saying of the Australians, who'd learned it from the British, was that there were only three things wrong with the Yanks: they were overpaid, oversexed and over here. There was certainly animosity between the Australian soldiers and the Americans. Quite often a bloke would be going out with a girl and a Yank would come along and try to steal her. You could see this all the time. The Australians' resentment often reached such a point that there'd be fights. On his way home from work one day Alec noticed an Australian soldier with his girlfriend, just strolling happily along, when two Yanks came up and tried to entice her away. They abused the Australian soldier and one of them threw a punch when he gave them some lip. The Aussie hit back, and the next thing Alec knew, four more Yanks had joined in.

It didn't take long before the Australian had flattened all six of them. Alec approached him and said, 'I was a Digger in the last war, and we sure weren't told how to stoush like that! Where did you do your basic training?' The soldier grinned. 'In a boxing stadium, Dig. Before I joined up.'

By this stage Nancy, Alec's eldest daughter, was teaching at a school up in Singleton, having become the first university graduate in the history of the Griffiths family by earning a Bachelor of Science. Each time she came down to visit on weekends the headmaster would say, 'I really don't know whether I want you to go down to Sydney, with those awful Yanks there. I'll come into school on Monday and find I haven't got a teacher.'

Much of the resentment towards the Americans came about because there was a general feeling that they had come into the war too late, especially in New Guinea — that they'd waited until the fighting was almost over before joining in. Australians couldn't understand why there were so many Aussies off fighting in New Guinea and yet so many Americans here pinching their girls. Alec wasn't alone in thinking it would have been better to have the Yanks up in New Guinea, fighting the Japs, and have Australians protecting Australia. It just seemed logical. And matters weren't helped when General Douglas MacArthur lavished praise on 'Allied' troops for their valiant exploits at Milne Bay and on capturing Kokoda. The fact that he was referring to the exploits of *Australian* troops — for example their capture of Kokoda in November 1942 — without singling them out really enraged the Diggers. And, remembering the Battle of Polygon Wood on the Western Front, it enraged Alec. The war years on the home front were not all animosity however. Alec and Effie loved the fact that they could listen to the radio every evening, and in some respects forget that there was a war on. They listened to Jack Davey's 'Hi ho everybody' and 'Mrs 'Obbs' on 2GB, 'Dad and Dave' on 2UW and 'The Horseleys in Horsetralia' on 2CH, among other things. True, they were just as likely to hear the BBC News War Review, propaganda plays on 2UW or Prime Minister Curtin (on *every* station) beseeching them to buy Austerity Loans to supply tanks and fighting planes for the war effort.

* * *

One Monday in April 1945, Alec was in the bathroom shaving before going to work. Nancy barged in and said, 'I'm going to get married Dad.'

'What a lot of rot,' he replied.

Nan wanted to get married to her boyfriend Peter Johnson while he was on leave from Borneo. 'It'll be this weekend, if they'll let him out.'

'Oh get away, you're too young to get married.'

But Nan would not give up. 'How old were *you* when you got married?'

She had him! He didn't relent; he simply had no comeback. He *had* married young, that day in November 1921, and had not regretted it one minute since. Not even when, on each of their wedding anniversaries, Effie would sneak up behind him and chant, 'Remember, Remember, the fifth of November ... gunpowder, treason and plot!'

And so, that weekend Nan and Peter got married. After a few days' honeymoon at Cronulla, Peter went back to the war and Nan went back to her school and showed the headmaster the wedding ring and said, 'Well, I still haven't gone off with one of the Yanks, but have a look at this!'

The headmaster couldn't believe it. For a second or two he was worried that Nan would resign and move back to Sydney. But then he remembered that teaching was a specified essential occupation. For as long as the war lasted there was no way in the world that Nan could get out of it. She loathed teaching at that school, mainly because it was so far away from her home in Sydney. Alec had often said to her, 'Just leave!', but that was impossible. He'd investigated the situation, and was prepared to pay off Nan's education bond, but you simply weren't allowed to skip off. You'd be put in gaol if you were in a protected essential occupation and didn't go to work.

The wharfies were also in a specified essential occupation. Many of them were held in the highest contempt because they went on strike so often. They wanted 'danger money', and they got it. Then they returned to work ... and went on strike again not long afterwards, wanting *more* money. And it often took them five days to load a ship. The Army — with half as many blokes working — would do it in two. The wharfies were responsible for ensuring that weapons, munitions and food got to the Australian boys who were fighting overseas, but often it got to them late simply because of the selfishness and the political bastardry of the wharfies. They were regarded as absolutely despicable — by Alec and his family, and by just about everybody else. But the union held the power on the wharves.

In July 1945, just a month or so before the war ended, Alec's dear mother Eliza Jane passed away peacefully at the age of 74.

She had endured much hardship in the early days, as a widow bringing up seven children on her own. Now she had gone to her rest with the children by her bedside. She deserved no less.

Alec hadn't expected the war to be as serious as the first one, but it had turned out to be pretty bad. The first Sydney to Hobart yacht race symbolised the return of peace. As Alec stood at Watson's Bay to watch the yachts gracefully and peacefully capturing the breeze, he remembered the earlier, more distant war. The war he had sailed across thousands of miles of ocean to get to, in the company of his best mate. The war he had returned home from alone. He hoped he would see more yachts, for many years to come.

CHAPTER TWENTY-TWO
The Inventor

With the war finished, Alec devoted more of his spare time to inventing. He had already built a caravan on the back of a truck, something that had never been done before, and had invented an electric wheelchair, of which he'd made a few. One day he got a telephone call from Joe B., who had been in the degaussing gang. 'Griff,' he said. 'I know you've made some electric wheelchairs for charity. I'd like you to do something for me if you could.'

'Sure, Joe,' Alec replied.

'My father lives up at Rockhampton, in north Queensland. He's an invalid and confined to a wheelchair. Before the war his friends used to drive him out to the cemetery each weekend so he could pay his respects to Mum. But they haven't been able to get petrol, and he has to make his own way out and back. It's a big hike — I don't reckon he can keep it up for much longer. His chair's fitted with a bike chain and a crank handle but he's finding it just too much. I'm off to Rocky in a couple of weeks and I'd love to be able to tell him we're doing something for him. But the chair's got to be good enough to handle the distance.'

'I'll think about it,' Alec promised. And he did.

The next time he saw Joe he said, 'When you go up north, make a few sketches and measurements so I can get an idea of what's needed.'

Joe was back in less than a week. Alec examined his very rough sketches and said, 'Now, what I need you to do is to go to a place where they hire out wheelchairs, select one that is nearest to your father's, and get them to deliver it to my place in Segenhoe Street.'

This was an easy task. With the large market of invalided soldiers returning from the war, there were plenty of wheelchairs on offer. Alec got all the necessary items and designed and made an electric motor to make the chair run. The kids had a great time, driving it up and down the back lane and giving it exhaustive tests. When it proved satisfactory, Alec returned the chair in its original condition to the hirer, and Joe later took the motor and mechanical gear up to Rockhampton, where he found they fitted perfectly on his father's chair. Before Joe left Rocky again his father made several successful trips out to the cemetery. Six months later Joe paid another visit up north and found the chair still going strong, though it had needed a new set of tyres (the original ones hadn't been designed for its newfound speeds). Alec built quite a few similar chairs for invalided soldiers, believing the men deserved a better go at life than the government had given their predecessors after World War I.

It soon became apparent that inventing was distracting Alec. One of Beryl's jobs was on Parramatta Road, in the office of a diamond merchant. She had an arrangement with her father that she would walk to Stanmore after work and wait to be picked up by him, on his way home from work. One day she was horrified to see Alec's ute go by with one of the bosses from Alec's work as a passenger, and making no attempt to stop for her. 'Dad's having a joke with me,' she said to herself. 'He'll turn around in a minute and come back for me.' It wasn't long before she realised that he was not coming back.

During the long trip home — exacerbated by the peak-hour rush — by tram and train, followed by the long walk from Arncliffe station, she became angrier and angrier. On arriving home she stormed into the house yelling, 'Where is he? Where *is* he?' Alec never heard the end of that. Ever.

But then things changed. He went from being distracted by his inventing, to being distracted from it when his son-in-law Peter came back from Borneo. Nan had decided that she and Peter had to find their own home, as the Griffiths house was bursting at the seams. She'd talked about 'squatting' in an empty house, as some people did, but her parents forbade it, and in any case the supply of empty houses soon dried up.

In the latter part of 1945, with Australian soldiers returning home, a huge shortage of housing began. At first the young couple wanted to rent a place, but rental housing was as rare as hen's teeth; they would have to buy. One day, after many weeks of unsuccessful searching, travelling out from the Griffiths home, they saw an advertisement for a house in Blakehurst. The ad said that it was being shown between eight-thirty and nine-thirty in the morning. Nan and Peter didn't care about that: waking up the rest of the household, they were off to Blakehurst by train before it even got light. In the darkness they propped themselves up against the gate to wait for the agent. By eight-thirty the entire street was full of people, all double-queued right down to the end and around the corner.

Nan and Peter looked around the house and asked the agent, 'How much key money do you want?'

'None,' he replied. 'I'm not into that sort of thing. This is dead straight.'

'Well,' they asked, 'when will we know if we've got a chance?'

The agent looked at them. 'You were here first. If you want to write out a cheque for the deposit, it's yours.'

The people behind them in the queue — hundreds of them — were devastated. Nan and Peter, needless to say, were overjoyed. A few days earlier they had thought they'd bought a house in Mosman, but it had fallen through. The price had been pegged and they paid a deposit. A day later they got a call from the agent. He didn't say that someone else had offered more money; just that the vendor had decided to withdraw the house from sale. Peter, who was now working as a bank officer, knew differently: someone else had come along and offered the agent a bribe. Agents weren't allowed to accept bribes, of course, but what a buyer might do was say, 'See that filthy old piece of carpet in the back room that isn't worth tuppence? Well, I'll give you a thousand pounds for that.' Or a blowfly on the wall might attract a premium of two thousand. This was a particularly nasty form of what was known as key money; in effect, black market money to get the key. It was a criminal offence to offer key money and you could be put in gaol. But due to a loophole in the law, you could get away with it because if you were challenged you'd say, 'I didn't pay that to get the house, I paid it for the fly on the wall.' Or whatever. Key money was a big factor in domestic life after the war. Not only did you normally have to have it in order to buy a house, you also had to be prepared to do an illegal thing. It was postwar law — the law of the streets.

Housing wasn't the only commodity in short supply. Building materials were also particularly difficult to come by, and initiative and resourcefulness became more important than finances in securing some of them. One day down on the harbour, Alec saw some men dumping dozens of concrete blocks over the sides of ships which were berthed at a wharf near Circular Quay. He asked them what was going on. They told him that as Japanese fighter planes had been particularly active in machine-gunning the bridges of Allied ships, a solid wall of concrete about three inches thick had been built right around the bridge and a concrete overhang built on top. This was done not only on the larger liners, but on the coastal steamers as well.

Concrete blocks about eighteen inches square were made, but instead of their edges being straight so that two blocks would slip together neatly, the makers cast half-holes in the edge of each block so that when two blocks were put together the two half-holes corresponded and allowed a large bolt to go through. The resultant rigid wall was virtually impenetrable to the enemy's bullets, and in this way many a ship was saved. Alec was impressed. He was also most keen on securing some of the blocks for himself, and asked if he could take some away with him. The men were glad to get rid of them. And so Alec brought the Bedford ute over from work and loaded it up until the guards were down over the tyres. Over the next few weekends the concrete blocks became the steps down to his workshop at the bottom of the backyard. Clothing, too, was still scarce, and much of it still rationed. If someone gave you two ration coupons as a wedding gift you'd be over the moon, for it was the most precious thing they could ever give. Nan had had to buy cheesecloth to make her nighties; it was the only material available. It was that or nothing when it came to a nightie. And it was so flimsy it might as well have been nothing. The night before her wedding, Nan had shown Effie her best cheesecloth nightie. Effie showed it to her mother, who was horrified. 'She'll wear a petticoat under it, won't she?' she asked. The trouble was that petticoats were themselves virtually nonexistent due to rationing. Most people didn't complain about the system, because it was all in a good cause: the needs of a nation at war and then recovering from it. The only people who complained about shortages seemed to be the very people who had plenty of everything, namely the black-marketeers. While most people had worked for the war effort, these people had in fact worked against it. After the war it became very clear to working families like the Griffithses just who these venal people had been. They were the ones who hadn't been able to rub two shillings together before the war, but who had now amassed such fortunes through black-marketeering that they could enthrone themselves in mansions in the posh Eastern Suburbs.

* * *

In mid-1950 the Korean War began. Australia was at it again, sending its boys off to fight in some part of the world where, many argued, they had no business being. This time Alec was not involved. Still energetic, he turned his hand to developing his cara-ute concept, improving the setup in a number of ways. Once he had completed the drawings and made sure any resulting vehicle could be registered, he patented the design under the Commonwealth of

Australia *Designs Act* and was entered on the Register of Designs (No. 37273) as the Owner thereof. He went into production, but Rockdale Council soon stopped him because they considered the work too industrial for a residential area.

Alec now had a new Vauxhall Velox utility, to which he had bolted the improved set-up. A photograph was taken at Carss Bush Park by a Vauxhall salesman, and it was published in *Wheels* magazine and also in *Popular Science* in the United States, where the caption read: 'Piggyback trailer. Here is a mobile home that rides on top of its car instead of being pulled along behind it. Designed especially for camping trips, it has full-sized adult beds on the lower level, bunks for youngsters on the upper, and room for luggage in the front. It is built in Australia for G.M. Vauxhall pick-ups, makes parking and reversing a cinch.' The American car industry was so impressed that production began there almost immediately, exploiting Alec's design. And, adding salt to the wound, when production of his cara-ute module commenced in Australia it was hailed as an American invention.

If he had had the money and the time Alec would have fought the car manufacturers in the courts. After all, the design could well have ensured a very comfortable future for his family. It was the beginning of what evolved into the multi-million dollar motorhome industry, and he was never to see a penny of it. The only recognition he would ever get came in 1981, when a certificate was presented to him at an inventors convention in Sydney. It read: 'Cara-ute. This invention was originally conceived in 1950 and was the first time a mounting of a caravan body on a utility truck was thought of. While today this is not a concept unknown to us, the inventor of this idea was the first in the world to conceive it. It has been conceived to a point where it is now in use universally.' But in 1950 Alec was very disappointed, though he never allowed himself to become bitter. That led nowhere. Instead of chasing his fortune, he decided to go full steam ahead with making self-propelled wheelchairs for disabled people.

One morning in 1951 he was out in the front garden when the

newspaper boy threw the paper into the garden and unintentionally hit him with it. Picking it up, Alec noticed that there was a rubber band around it — a rolled-up paper was easier for the boy to throw. Before this, he had always simply put a twist in it, which meant that you ended up with very crumpled reading matter. Alec looked at the boy, who started to apologise.

'That's all right,' Alec said. 'I like the way you've put a band around the paper.'

'Yeah,' the boy said, 'but you've got no flamin' idea what a job it is.'

Alec's mind ticked over immediately. 'So you haven't got a machine for it?'

'No, we 'aven't. But it'd be just the shot.'

Alec went inside and thought about what the boy had said. He concluded that wrapping the newspaper would be better than using a rubber band, even though he hadn't seen it done before. So, in what was left of his 'spare time', he set about designing and building a newspaper wrapping machine. The idea was that the newspapers would go into the machine flat, and a mechanical system would then roll them up and wrap them in brown paper. He could never get hold of enough copies locally to perfect the machine, so he started going into the newspaper office in town at four in the morning to get a batch of them. Each time he did this he remembered cycling over to the *Herald* office as a boy and picking up the paper with its news on the Great War. The papers he was picking up now also headlined war news.

Eventually, Alec patented the world's first newspaper wrapping machine (Patent No. 153740, dated 1 August 1951). He sold the machine and the production rights to a newsagency down the road. He couldn't sell it to other paper shops because it was only possible to sell the rights to one person. The proprietor was very happy with the deal, and when production started, Alec was to get around six pounds for every machine made.

He never got a penny.

The proprietor was the cobber of a local publican, and the

publican had a relative who was the superintendent engineer of a shipping company. This man was intended to organise the manufacturing of the machine, but was shortly sent back to England to oversee the building of a ship. Consequently the planned production didn't go ahead.

Not long after this a visitor came out to see Alec — another engineer, employed at a paper works. He wanted Alec to scrub the agreement with the newsagency proprietor and offered a lot more in the way of royalties.

'I can't,' Alec said. 'It's already signed.'

'Well, do you mind if I see the machine running?'

Alec took him to the little shed and demonstrated the wrapping operation. The engineer was visibly astonished as he watched the papers going through. With a pleased look, he said, 'Well, I can build a paper wrapping machine now.'

And that's exactly what he did. He ended up selling scores of them — almost exact copies of Alec's machine — and made a small fortune. Years later, he died. His son, who had read an article about Alec being the inventor of the machine, wrote to Alec disputing the claim made in the article. But when, after a few letters, Alec sent him a copy of the patent he finally admitted, to Alec and to himself, that his father had got the idea from that visit to a small shed at Segenhoe Street.

CHAPTER TWENTY-THREE
Autumn Leaves

Fleetingly I saw the stranger passing by — the camera's eye
In the Anzac March. Not swinging along as he would wish,
Nor was he huddled down in the Land Rover
More, was he like some proud warrior, with a victor's wave, between the wars.
I heard the commentator speak his name:
One of the last of the Australian Flying Corps, he said.
And in that instant, with my uncle's image in my heart, a metamorphosis occurred
And captured that warrior's name, his style, his life, as if
An urgent message had been sent from Abe.
Both Alec and Abe joined the Army, transferred to the Australian Flying Corps,
Trod parallel paths in foreign lands ... but never met.
I wish they'd met. I know they will.

Nola Fisher, 'In Passing' (Dedicated to Albert S. Pettit and Alec Griffiths of the Australian Flying Corps)

Alec retired in 1965, at the age of 65, after 45 years' service as an electrical fitter at Coupland & Waddell. It was only then that he started doing things just for himself. Every

Wednesday, he and an old mate would head out on Botany Bay together to do some fishing. Alec's boat had two engines on it for safety — a twenty horsepower unit and a seven horsepower one — because when the wind gets up on Botany Bay it really can blow a gale. And did they get some fish then!

In October 1968 Effie and Alec decided to have a holiday in New Zealand. It was time for Alec to fly in a plane again. He'd never particularly wanted to, even back in the days when occasionally he'd had to go down to Rose Bay to meet his sister-in-law Alice coming in from New Zealand on a Qantas or Tasman Empire Airways flying boat. He didn't know how they got those things up into the sky; they were like a big boat with wings. And out on Rose Bay, when a few of them were moored there, they looked for all the world like white swans sitting on the water.

On landing at Christchurch, after a flight that staggered Alec with its speed and smoothness, he and Effie were taken by car to their hotel. The next day they boarded a coach for a tour of the South Island. The tour guide produced a microphone and invited the passengers to introduce themselves. When Effie and Alec explained how they'd first met, a loud cheer went up throughout the entire coach. In Queenstown they booked into a charming hotel overlooking the mountains and the lake. In the morning they took a boat trip on an old steamer and went up the lake to visit a sheep farm. The day after that they continued on to The Bluff, at the southernmost tip of the South Island. During a restful evening Effie and Alec talked about how they would celebrate their 47th wedding anniversary in a few days' time. The rest of the coach group had already been making plans for them all to have a big party when they got back to Christchurch.

The following day's itinerary included a boat trip out to sea, but Effie didn't want to go because she was afraid of getting seasick. So she and Alec went for a walk along the shore, just the two of them. They reminisced about Bob Lauchland and how he had brought them together. Alec was the happiest man on earth — as he'd been ever since his lovely Effie wrote to say 'Yes!' all those years ago.

After breakfast the next morning they were sitting in their room when Effie suddenly put her hand to her chest and said, 'Ooh, for a moment I thought I was going to have a heart attack!' She smiled at Alec and he knew everything was all right. A few moments later she got up, took three steps towards the washbasin, and collapsed in the corner of the room.

Alec jumped to his feet to help her, uncertain of what to do. After a second or two he raced out to the reception desk, but there was no one there. Frantic, he found another guest, who followed him back to the room. Together they lifted Effie onto the bed. Still unable to find any of the hotel staff, Alec called an ambulance, which had to come from Invercargill, over 30 miles away.

At the hospital, he saw his whole life as if he were looking down a tunnel. At the other end — the shining end — was Effie's radiant, smiling face. The light dimmed when a doctor came up and informed Alec that his wife had had a cerebral haemorrhage, and that nothing could be done for her.

Alec sat alone in the ward with Effie. When he saw signs that she was dying he pressed the call button frantically. No one came. He ran out looking for someone — a doctor, a nurse, anyone — but the corridors were empty. Eventually he found the staff in the dining room, having lunch. He called to them for help but no words came. He went back to Effie and was with her, by her side and holding her hand, when she died at midday.

His brothers Fred and Lock had also passed away — within four days of each other — only two years earlier, and his youngest brother Jack had died of a cerebral haemorrhage in 1964. Now, Alec hoped that he would soon wake up and find that all this had been a bad dream. He consoled himself a little by telling himself how happy Effie would have been, passing away in a town with such similarities to Scotland. The grief and sadness lingered for a long time, but for Alec retired life went on.

One day the people living across the road came over and said, 'We've got a friend who was in the Australian Flying Corps. We'd like to introduce you to him.' Intrigued, and looking forward to comparing stories, Alec joined them. As soon as he laid eyes on the man he said, 'Ah, yes. Arthur Hemmings! G'day Tiny, how are you?' They hadn't seen each other since 1917. He and Alec had been living within a mile of each other for 60 years and neither of them had even known if the other had survived the Great War. They now resolved to keep in contact, which they did in part by attending meetings of the Australian Society of World War One Aero Historians. Both Arthur and Alec even led the Anzac Day march in Sydney, in the company of the State governor.

By early 1993 a very good mate of Alec's, Eric Watson, had been taking them off to the society for almost a couple of decades. On the way to one meeting he said to Alec, 'You know, it's a shame that the AFC Association doesn't exist any more.'

'But it does,' Alec replied.

'It does?' Eric was incredulous. 'No, it can't possibly be ... Well, if it does, who's the president?'

'He's sitting in the back seat.'

Eric was dumbfounded. 'Who, Arthur?'

'Yes.'

'So what are you?,' returned Eric.

'Well, I'm the vice-president,' Alec confessed. Even though there were now only two office bearers left, constitutionally they were the AFC Association.

'So how come Arthur got to be president and you're only vice-president?'

There was a chuckle in the back seat.

'Oh,' Alec replied. 'Arthur's older than me.' He'd figured that any AFC bloke older than 93 deserved to be the president.

Still getting over the shock, Eric asked, 'So where do you have your association meetings?'

'In your car, on the way to the society.'

Arthur died not long after that. Eric said to Alec, 'Well, you're promoted now. You're the president.' It was true. Alec had become the president of a society of valiant men of the Australian Flying Corps; a society whose members were all dead except for Alec, and a Queenslander, Harold Edwards, with whom Alec kept in touch by telephone.

In autumn, a short time after he had observed his 75th Anzac Day in Australia, Alec was taken to an RAAF base and shown over an F-18 Hornet. The Air Force people put him inside the cockpit and showed him all the complex instruments. 'Absolutely above my head,' he said. But the officers fussed over him and filled his head with figures. The F-18 could do 2500 kilometres an hour or something like that ... all Alec could think of was the poor old SE5a that people had said in 1917 would be the fastest plane ever to fly. It did 130 miles an hour. The officers, on learning he had been in the Flying Corps, assumed that he had been a pilot. 'No,' Alec said with a twinkle, 'I was mostly *under* the ground!'

Oddly enough, on a very moving visit to the Australian War Memorial in Canberra, Alec came across an SE5a biplane. One of the curators proceeded to tell him that the machine-gun on the side of the fuselage was able to fire bullets through the revolving propeller without hitting it. 'Yes,' Alec said, 'that's the Constantinesco Synchronising Gear. It worked on hydraulics.' He looked at the ceiling, as though recalling information for a school exam. 'Although they used it quite a lot, it wasn't exactly a success. The main trouble was, the gun was always a fair distance from the propeller. Now, the charge in the bullets used to vary, and if one of them had less charge it was slower getting to the propeller and the timing was wrong — so the bullet went smack through a propeller blade. They used to have a testing bay where they'd set the planes up, put the propellers on, and set the CSG. But that was the main trouble — the variations in the charge. It was the same with artillery shells. That's why so many came down on our own trenches.' The man looked at Alec in amazement, thinking he'd at last found someone else with a passion for the SE5a. When Alec said that the only reason for his knowledge was that he'd been at the squadron where the first plane of this type was introduced, the man almost fell over.

* * *

Alec heard that year that the federal government was sending a commemorative mission to the Western Front, so he put his hand up. There were over 200 applications, though only two from each State would get to go. The physical and mental assessments that the applicants had to undergo were very strict — it was like trying to enlist all over again. The old boys were even fitted with slouch hats, just as Alec had been in 1916. Only this time nobody minded when he tried a few on before he found one that fitted him.

At a ceremony at Victoria Barracks, the Veterans Affairs minister, John Faulkner, read out the names of the veterans who would be going on the pilgrimage. Alec's name was on the list. Tears welled in his eyes: no one knew whether they were tears of sadness or tears of joy. In 1918, when he left those awful fields in Belgium and France, he had never wanted to go back again. He also knew that, to fulfil his dream, one day he would have to.

Once he'd been selected to join the mission he located his old VPK camera which he had taken aboard the *Hororata* in 1916 and developed the film. Developing the photographs entailed leaving the daylight paper out in the sun for a certain time. Considering the film had been undeveloped for almost 80 years, they didn't come out too badly. There, staring back at him from the deck of an old ship, stood a familiar sixteen-year-old lad, wearing a peaked cap. In another frame, Bob Lauchland and a handful of other young lads in khaki smiled back as they tossed a Christmas dinner into the South Atlantic. Alec remembered their larrikin antics. He heard their laughter. He saw their death.

Now, he broke a little of his 75 years of silence on what he had seen in France and Belgium. In the intervening years he had talked openly enough about what he did during the war, but never about what he *saw*. He could never bring himself to do that, until now. He had always held the belief that unless you'd lived through the horrors of the Western Front you could never understand. The whole thing had been a complete shambles — a disaster — tempered only by the valour, the raw courage, of the men who fought in it. And by their selfless devotion to their mates.

The night before the group was to leave Australia for the 75th anniversary of the end of 'the war to end all wars' they stayed at the Lady Davidson Repatriation Hospital in Turramurra, on Sydney's North Shore. Their special ward was called 'Western Front HQ'. Farewelling them, Prime Minister Paul Keating said, 'My generation of Australians, all Australians, are in your debt.' It had been a long time coming, but finally a politician, with no political agenda in mind, had humbly thanked the Diggers for what they had done. And a wellwisher in the crowd at the Town Hall yelled out, 'Watch out for those French girls!' One of the old boys grinned and called back, 'That's all we *can* do now.'

CHAPTER TWENTY-FOUR
Answering the Call Again

They spent the first day in Paris, where they attended a commemorative ceremony in the shadows of the majestic Arc de Triomphe. As the haunting notes of 'The Last Post' floated in the air, the first tears were shed. Alec stood at attention — as he had done so many years before at Rouelles just before being separated from Bob — and then laid a wreath of Australian wildflowers and gum leaves on France's Tomb of the Unknown Warrior. It was late August; tourists thronged the city. The original intention had been to have the veterans' visit coincide with Armistice Day, but it was felt that some of them might not survive the coming European winter. Alec reckoned that if he had survived it in the icy trenches and dugouts in 1917, he would have survived it in comfortable hotels in 1993, but he wasn't going to kick up a fuss. He was here.

* * *

The old Diggers now left Paris for Villers-Bretonneux, on the Somme. Once more, Australian Diggers were going off to battlefields on the other side of the world. Seventy-five years on, they were answering the call again. Sitting in the coach with the others, Alec recalled being told in November 1918: 'We've won the war!' It was nonsense, Alec reflected. We did not win the war. Neither did the Germans. No, it was war itself that had won. War always would.

As far as he could tell, the Great War had been fought for the gratification of the European monarchies and governments. The politicians in their swank offices and the brass-hats sweeping their hands across battle maps in their French chateaux had just been playing marbles with men's lives. Alec hadn't really thought this at the time. He had simply thought, 'Well, the Army said we gotta do this, and that's it.' And he believed that, while the Kaiser might have got things all wrong from the outset, there should have been other ways of rectifying things once the killing started. The men who could have done something about the slaughter could have stopped it all with the stroke of a pen.

Before he had gone off to the Great European War, war had seemed somehow heroic to Alec. Thrilling, and downright adventurous. When he got to it, he learnt that there was no glory in war. Heroism perhaps. And mateship. Courage, honour, selflessness, endurance and sacrifice. But no glory.

What there had been was a horrid wastage of young life, executed in an arena of devastation, filth and misery. Over the years many Anzacs had told Alec stories about how they had eventually grown accustomed to the colourless, treeless, stinking, corpse-strewn waste of the Western Front. Alec had not, and he never would. The horrific images, the noise and the memories of the smell, never left him. He simply chose not to share them.

Even 50 years after the Great War, Alec had known of women who had never married because their fiance or their sweetheart had been killed in France or Belgium. And as a veteran he knew all the casualty figures. The total butcher's bill for the Western Front was more than 3 000 000 men killed in three years. They had enlisted in their thousands, and in their thousands they had been slaughtered. Almost 420 000 Australians enlisted — every single one of them a volunteer — representing almost half of the eligible Australian men who could have joined. Theirs was the only completely volunteer army in the Great War. Of these, 330 000 fought in the killing fields of foreign lands. Almost 230 000 of them became casualties, giving Australia the highest casualty rate per capita of the Allied forces.

Of all Australians who fought, two-thirds were killed or wounded. And of these 230 000, almost 60 000 were killed. The Western Front battles, in which for six months Alec had taken part, alone claimed 46 000 of these men. Huge numbers of men had been slaughtered while gaining — or losing — a few yards of foreign mud. Many of them had been slaughtered before Alec's very eyes.

* * *

The veterans swept into Villers-Bretonneux to be welcomed by a kangaroo painted on a sign reading, in French: 'Villers-Bretonneux was twinned with Robinvale, Victoria, in 1984.' The main town square was Place Robinvale and a nearby park was named Place Melbourne. Two of the main roads were Rue de Melbourne and Rue Victoria, so named, they were told, since 1923. At the Australian National Memorial just outside Villers-Bretonneux on the road to Fouilloy, Alec's room-mate, Bill Davies, embarked on his quest to find a grave — any Australian grave at all — that carried the name of his unit. He had 800 graves to choose from. His aim was to plant an Australian flag, which he did. 'There will never be enough flags to go round,' he said, 'to measure all the emotion we have.' Another member of the group, Ted Smout, found it almost impossible to comprehend the sheer number of names inscribed on the memorial. He was confronted with almost 11 000 of them.

Following a wreath-laying ceremony and the unveiling of a battlefield plaque, the veterans attended a function in the primary school in Villers-Bretonneux itself. Above the school was a little museum full of photographs and artefacts. And above the blackboard in every classroom was a plaque that read, again in French: 'Never Forget Australia.'

From Villers-Bretonneux the old men went to Pozières where, in 1916, the Australians suffered more than 23 000 casualties while advancing the front line one mile. And here, as the Windmill battlefield plaque was unveiled, the Somme earth became damp once more with Australian tears.

After a rest day the group visited the Australian cemetery at VC Corner, Fromelles, before heading up to Belgium. They went to

Tyne Cot, situated between Zonnebeke and Passchendaele. In Tyne Cot, the largest Commonwealth war cemetery in the world, lie almost 12 000 men. Of these graves more than 8300 bear no name. The shellfire in the battles was so intense that individual identification of the dead was impossible. Behind the graves, on a wall, are the names of a further 35 000 who have no known resting place. These names, Alec was told, were to have joined the others inscribed on the Menin Gate, but after 55 000 names had been put there, there was no more space. Alec was one of the few visitors to the Western Front since Armistice Day who did not find these figures hard to believe.

Of the graves at Tyne Cot around 1300 are Australian. Many of these men were killed in October 1917 during the Battle of Broodseinde, a battle in which Alec took part. During the fighting, Australians captured all the blockhouses that now formed much of the cemetery. It took Alec about five minutes to hobble from the first blockhouse to the second. In October 1917, it took the Australians five days.

The party of old men travelled east along Zonnebeke Road to Polygoneveld. Those steady enough on their feet ascended the mound to pay tribute at the 5th Australian Division Memorial in Polygon Wood, where so very long ago — and yet not so long ago — artillery fire had churned up the ground into a morass. The memorial stands watch over almost 600 Australian graves, more than 400 of which bear no name. The thick forest of Polygon Wood now made it one of the most serenely beautiful places Alec had ever seen. Nonetheless, he could not rid his mind of the image of it in 1917: just craters and splintered stumps.

At Ypres the weary group attended a ceremony at the Menin Gate. Here 55 000 men named have no known grave. More than 6000 of them were Australians. At the ceremony the Australian military band played 'Waltzing Matilda' as it marched from the Great Cloth Hall to the Menin Gate. 'Advance Australia Fair' was then played, and Alec met the mayor of Ieper and the mayor of Passchendaele. The Cloth Hall had been rebuilt and the state in which Alec now saw it had to be much, much closer to the medieval original than the battered ruin he'd seen in 1917 when these men of the 1st AIF had passed through the old Menin Gate. Now, as the solemn words of 'Abide With Me' echoed around the walls, the old men retraced their steps. They limped, they hobbled, they were aided by their carers. But they retraced *their* steps. Alec wryly noted that the members of the Honour Guard provided by the Australian Army for the ceremony were young enough to be his grandchildren.

In the next few days the group went to Bullecourt, Mont St Quentin, Peronne and Bellenglise. At Bullecourt, they were told, local school children sing 'Waltzing Matilda' and occasionally write cards to the fallen Diggers who rest there. Bullecourt was an especially poignant place for one of the veterans. Howard Pope, who had served there with the 27th Battalion in 1917, recalled how the surrounding towns and villages had been razed and how the fields had become a quagmire covered with unburied bodies. These were images that would never leave him.

At Villers-Bretonneux, at Tyne Cot and at the Menin Gate, Alec saw the names of 18 000 *Australian* dead who have no known grave. He realised then, more than ever before, that Passchendaele and the Western Front deserve at least as much of a place in the Australian consciousness as Gallipoli holds. He didn't wish to take anything away from the Anzacs who fought at Gallipoli — some of whom later became good mates of his — but he knew that for every Australian soldier killed at Gallipoli, six were killed on the Western Front. And men who had fought at Gallipoli in 1915 and at the Somme in 1916 maintained that the shelling at the Somme was far worse. And Passchendaele eclipsed them all: it was the worst battlefield in history. At Passchendaele, many infantrymen considered an order to assault through the mud as a death sentence, as had the gunners in the batteries who were ordered to serve the guns until the last man fell. Yet many men had prayed for just such orders. Historians later opined that if you'd endured Passchendaele, it was a case of 'enough said'.

At one stage of the tour Alec piped up and asked their escorts, 'Where can we find a windmill near a coal mine?' They went to a lot of trouble to find it for him, and eventually they did. For a few hours he left the main bus convoy and his guide took him to the area he had landed in with Wrigley all those years ago. The fosse was now a huge mountain of tailings from the coal mine, but the area was still very much recognisable. Of course, the dugout was long gone, and the windmill had been destroyed. Alec spent a quiet moment here, and returned to the main convoy.

As the coach continued its journey, Alec began to discover how much of the Western Front he'd seen all those years ago. Wireless operators working with the artillery were certainly moved around a lot. Some of the places he recognised easily; others seemed changed, as if in disguise. It was like being used to a tattered black-and-white photograph of something, only to have it suddenly replaced by a brilliant colour shot. Often the colour was a fresh green, where fields of sugar beet had covered over the trenches and dugouts. But while Alec grappled with the scenes outside the coach window a different image kept recurring in his mind. He could not shut out the unearthly sight of wounded horses and mules struggling on stump-lined tracks or half-buried in shell craters. He saw the horse teams desperately trying to get the guns through, fighting their way through the mud, as though it were yesterday.

And he remembered Bob Lauchland, as the coach passed by fields whose corners were ablaze with red poppies. He heard the whispers of the men of a thousand battalions and gun batteries who lay beneath them. It made him wonder if he'd still go off to war if it were 1916 again. Like many elderly men he had acquired the habit of talking aloud to himself, and in a moment or two he heard the reply. 'I'm not sorry I joined up. I reckon it was the making of me.'

* * *

After what seemed a second lifetime Alec and his carers arrived at Dickebusch. Alec had passed through here frequently on his way to different batteries; now he was here on a personal mission. During the war Dickebusch had come to mean 'rest' for the Australian soldiers. Now it was the place of eternal rest for one Australian soldier in particular. Throughout his life Alec had dreamed

Alec at Bob's grave

many dreams but for three-quarters of a century he'd had one dream above all: to find the grave of his best mate and to say the farewell he'd never had the chance to say.

Silent and purposeful, through a field of chalky white, he shuffled. He glided to a halt as he found the object for which he had been searching. The journey here had been long, the route trying. The mud of the track that led here had covered his feet for 75 years.

There were no tears. No. The spongy soil of this land was already soaked through with tears, and could bear no more. Before him, the earth divulged its long-kept secret. There, in the Huts Cemetery at Dickebusch, among row upon chalky row of silent white headstones, he found Bob Lauchland's grave. The headstone was inscribed: 'Till the day dawns and the shadows fly away.'

'He's been here for 75 years,' Alec said to the few people present, and yet to no one. In silence they looked at him. 'The mateship we had ... it was exceptional. Having known Bob has influenced my whole life. If I'd never been mates with Bob, I would never have met and fallen in love with Effie and my entire life from 1917 would have been completely different. I thought I'd never find him, I never expected to do it. This is the *ultimate* ... the finale to a long life.' Alec had fulfilled his long dream; he had completed his pilgrimage. He'd been faithful to the rule of his life: Never say die until a dead horse kicks you.

Alec Griffiths planted an Australian flag on the grave. It felt as though he had simply put his hand on his mate's shoulder. He could see Bob's face there, as vivid as ever. Silent words of farewell passed between them.

It was the first time an Australian flag had been put on that grave. No one, including Bob's relatives, had known where he was buried. Straightening up, with his hand on his heart, Alec spoke the words that should never need to be uttered — but always will be, so long as there is war. With the headstone in front of him he whispered, 'Lest we forget.'

But words are never enough.

Afterword

by Nan Bennett

In a way it seemed that every day of my father's long and happy life had been leading towards the moment when he found Bob's grave. The heartache of their separation had lingered with him — haunted him — for over 75 years. He told me afterwards that when he looked down at the grave he saw Bob's face, as clearly as if Bob himself was there, and felt the burden lift.

He endeared himself to all those who were his companions on that nostalgic trip back to the Western Front. Two men whom he and I met and befriended before his departure were Murray Olds, from 2UE, and Christopher Tuckfield, writer and director of the film *Cenotaph*. Both Murray and Christopher assured me that they would keep an eye on Dad over in France and Belgium, and that they would also do all they could to help him achieve his overwhelming ambition, to find this grave and say goodbye to Bob. After he returned to Australia, my father spoke with great affection of these two men, as he did of his carers, headed by Judy Bush. Every single one of those people who accompanied those old Diggers deserves our admiration and our gratitude.

The trip itself took a lot out of those mature men and women.

However, I don't believe that any one of them would voluntarily have forgone the opportunity to attend. For my father, it was something he was *destined* to do.

My father was a man of great integrity, honesty, humility and compassion, qualities that my parents were determined to instil in their children. We enjoyed a happy childhood, confident in our parents' devotion to each other. Encouraged to achieve our ambitions, we were told not to sit back and wait for things to happen. 'Never wait for handouts, and always consider the other fellow,' my father always said.

It was Dad's tenacity of purpose that embarked me on the quest to find someone who could tell the story of my father's life. I searched high and low without success, and during this search I did not encounter a single person to whom I was confident that I could entrust the responsibility. Had I not inherited his 'never give up' spirit I think I may have abandoned the idea, some time into the unfruitful search. However, his favourite saying, 'Never say die until a dead horse kicks you', kept swirling around in my head. I could not give up! I had to find the person who could do it.

When I first spoke to Rob, after he had paid a visit to Dad to interview him for a newspaper article he wished to write, I felt by instinct that at last I had found the right person. Rob was the one. When Dad and I offered him the chance to do it, I think he also felt that he was the one. We arranged a protracted visit to Dad's home in Arncliffe to enable them to get to know one another. Their rapport was instant, and they developed an almost 'grandfather and grandson' relationship.

Up until now, my father had seldom allowed himself to speak of what he called 'the unspeakable'. He had told quite a few stories about what he had done in the Great War, but had spoken very little of what he had *seen*. For more than 75 years, most of his war experiences had remained locked in his memory. Now, Dad poured out his heart to Rob, and gave him the key. He opened up to Rob with countless recollections, never before related to anyone. During weeks and weeks of interviews, there was plenty of laughter in the

Segenhoe Street house. There was an abundance of tears, too. On both sides of the table.

After my father returned from France, he was immeasurably happy that he had done the seemingly impossible, and found Bob. His life, it seemed, was fulfilled. However, there was one more achievement that he coveted.

He had learnt of the intention to bring the Unknown Soldier from France and reverently lay him to rest in a place of honour in Canberra, on Remembrance Day 1993. My father so hoped to be part of this ceremony, perhaps so that, symbolically, he too could lay his best mate to rest. Dad was invited, and the invitation also extended to my husband Fred and myself. I could not think of a more appropriate ceremony for the three of us to attend.

In 1980, ten years after the death of my first husband Peter, I met up with Fred Bennett. Interestingly, in his possession Fred had a piece of Amy Johnson's aeroplane. Upon landing in Brisbane, Amy Johnson's plane had hit a barbed-wire fence that separated the Eagle Farm flying field from a cornfield, and had toppled over. Amy gave a fragment of the badly damaged wings of her aeroplane to the man who looked after the Eagle Farm airfield. This man, who, with his faithful horse Anzac, mowed the grass of the flying field and shooed livestock away when planes were landing, was Andy Lauchland. Andy — who was wounded five times and won the Military Medal serving in the AIF in the Great War — was Bob Lauchland's brother. The piece of the aeroplane wreckage was later given to Bob and Andy's sister, Jean.

Jean's daughter, Win, was my husband Fred's first wife, who had passed away in 1979. For my father, in seeing his daughter marry the widower of Bob Lauchland's niece, another bond with Bob had been forged.

Dad was so excited. Our departure was scheduled for a Monday. At his request, we had arranged to go by train rather than by plane. Despite his fascination with aviation, he regarded flying as his least favourite method of transport.

The day before our departure, Dad telephoned me.

'I've had a stroke,' he said, matter-of-factly.

'Where are you? Are you in hospital?'

'No.'

'Hang up. I will call an ambulance and meet you at the hospital.'

'I've had the ambulance, but I declined to go to the hospital with them,' he said. 'I wonder if you and Fred would still take me down to Canberra?'

Despite being completely paralysed on one side and partially paralysed on the other, we reluctantly agreed to the trip although it was insisted that he travel by plane. He revelled in this trip to Canberra and did his best to ignore the paralysis, which became quite a challenge for us when he insisted on sleeping in the upstairs bedroom of the rented apartment. Eventually we were able to leave his wheelchair at the foot of the stairs and manhandle him up them, but it took four people.

The next morning I went in to wake Dad up. He looked at me and asked if I would go to a hardware shop and get some lengths of pipe. He wanted to attach them to his legs to assist him to walk. Instead of getting the pipe, however, we took him to the local hospital where they fitted him with splints.

On the day of the ceremony he scorned the idea of taking the wheelchair along. He wanted to walk; he wanted to have with him the walking stick he had carved while on the Western Front. To reach his seat of honour he had to negotiate many steps, but with the assistance of some Red Cross helpers we were able to manoeuvre him to the allocated seats opposite the prime minister, Mr Paul Keating. My father took in every minute of the moving ceremony, reflecting on those who had not found their loved ones and the importance to the nation of the return of the Unknown Soldier. I am sure he was also thinking of Bob Lauchland.

However, it was after the ceremony that, for us, the most moving moment of all occurred. We had insisted on borrowing one of the Australian War Memorial wheelchairs to show Dad around the museum. Everywhere we went, in and around the War Memorial, he was approached by people. Especially young people. My father had a great deal of time for young people, and had devoted much of his time in his later years to educating school students on some of the horrors of the Great War, in the hope that they might take steps to safeguard the future from such horrors recurring. Now, in Canberra, dozens of boys and girls — mostly in their teens or younger — came up to the wheelchair, stood to attention, and looked Dad in the eye and said such things as, 'Could I shake your hand? I want to thank you for what you did for us, all those years ago. We, our generation, owe our freedom to you. Thank you.' It was all very unexpected, and most emotional and gratifying.

We returned from Canberra, and although Dad was still enjoying life immensely with his customary enthusiasm, I began to suspect that he felt he had achieved all his ambitions and wouldn't mind going to join Effie and Bob.

On 18 March 1995 my father suffered a second stroke. The following day he lapsed into a coma, from which he never recovered.

I regard this as how he would think of his passing:

My task accomplished and the long day done,
My wages taken, and in my heart
Some late lark singing,
Let me be gathered to the quiet west
The sundown splendid and serene — Death.
Anon.

Acknowledgments

For their invaluable assistance, support and encouragement (not to mention patience and understanding) spanning several years I would like to thank the following:

Fred Bennett
Nan Bennett
Andrew Crack
Catharine Crack
Sally Crack
John Klooster
Ricky Pfeiffer
Nick Bolton
Lambis Englezos
Paul Corby
Kurt Smyth
David Cantwell
Kate Kenefick
Derek White
Sharon McCarthy
Nola Fisher
Lois Carrington

And special thanks to the late Eric Watson of the Australian Society of World War One Aero Historians.

Excerpts from the poem 'The Crossley Tender' are reproduced with the kind permission of the author, Derek White, and the Australian Society of World War One Aero Historians.

Excerpts from the poem 'In Passing', dedicated to Albert S. Pettit and Alec Griffiths of the Australian Flying Corps, are reproduced with the kind permission of the author, Nola Fisher.

Above all, I would like to thank Alec Griffiths for his friendship. My life is all the more meaningful for having known him.

Index